I0446036

The Leica M Photographer

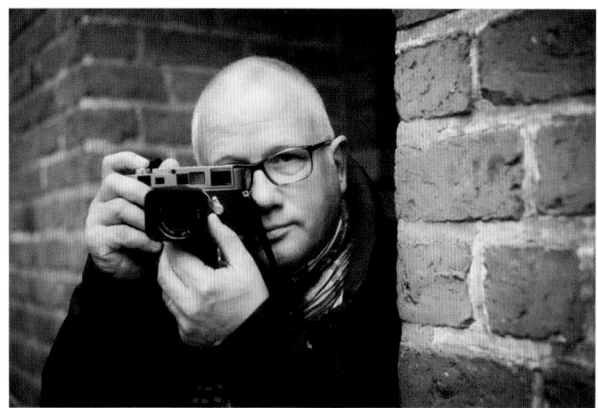

Foto: Katja Solcher

While studying medicine, Bertram Solcher worked as freelance photojournalist for regional and national newspapers, as well as national and international magazines. For the last 10 years he has worked in public relations and corporate photography, with a focus on medicine and science. While Solcher uses DSLR cameras for his commercial work, he uses the Leica M for projects that involve photographing people because the camera enables him to merge into the environment, allowing him to capture a very honest sense of reality in his images.

Solcher has been an enthusiastic Leica M photographer for the last 35 years, and has worked with almost all Leica M models, both analog and digital. He is an appointed member of the German Society for Photography, and has been an actively involved board member of the "Freelens" photographer's association. His current photography project, called "German Angst," is sponsored by a grant from the VG Bild-Kunst association.

Bertram Solcher

The LEICA M Photographer

Photographing with Leica's Legendary Rangefinder Cameras

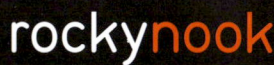

Library of Congress Cataloging-in-Publication Data

Solcher, Bertram.
The Leica M photographer : photographing with Leica's legendary
rangefinder cameras / Bertram Solcher. -- 1st edition.
     pages cm
ISBN 978-1-937538-62-0 (hardbound : alk. paper)
1. Leica camera. 2. Cameras. 3. Photography. I. Title.
TR263.L4S65 2015
771.3--dc23

2014045156

Editor: Joan Dixon
Copyeditor: Vanessa McVay
Layout: Cora Banek, www.artepictura.de
Cover Design: Helmut Kraus, www.exclam.de
Printed in China

ISBN: 978-1-937538-62-0

1st Edition 2015
© 2015 Bertram Solcher

Rocky Nook, Inc.
802 E. Cota Street, 3rd Floor
Santa Barbara, CA 93103

Copyright © 2015 by dpunkt.verlag GmbH, Heidelberg, Germany.
Title of the German original: Der Leica M Fotograf
German ISBN: 978-3-86490-204-8
Translation Copyright © 2015 by Rocky Nook. All rights reserved.

www.rockynook.com

All rights reserved. No part of the material protected by this copyright
notice may be reproduced or utilized in any form, electronic or
mechanical, including photocopying, recording, or by any information
storage and retrieval system, without written permission of the publisher.

Many of the designations in this book used by manufacturers and sellers
to distinguish their products are claimed as trademarks of their respective
companies. Where those designations appear in this book, and Rocky
Nook was aware of a trademark claim, the designations have been
printed in caps or initial caps. All product names and services identified
throughout this book are used in editorial fashion only and for the benefit
of such companies with no intention of infringement of the trademark.
They are not intended to convey endorsement or other affiliation with
this book.

While reasonable care has been exercised in the preparation of this
book, the publisher and author assumes no responsibility for errors or
omissions, or for damages resulting from the use of the information
contained herein or from the use of the discs or programs that may
accompany it.

This book is printed on acid-free paper.

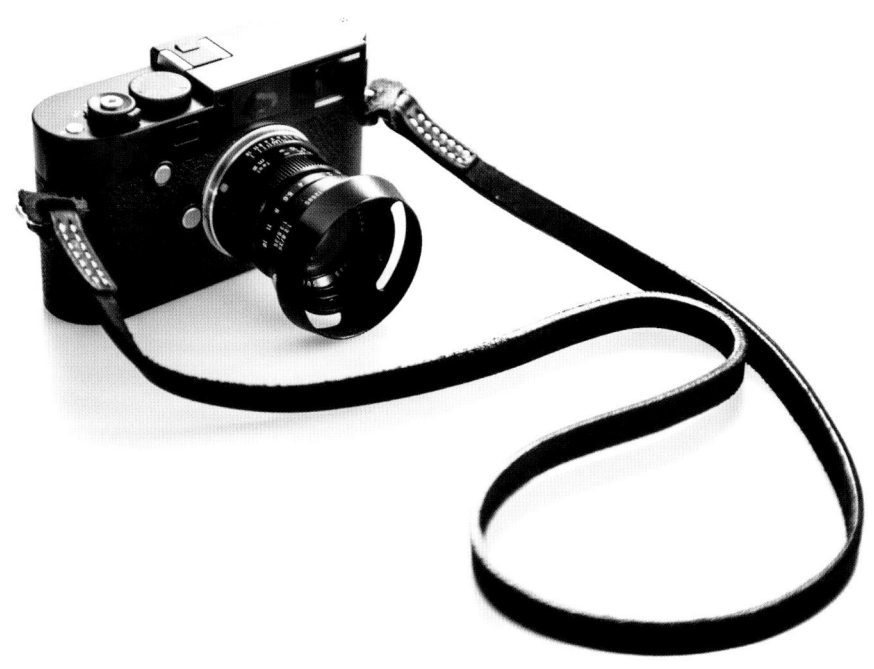

Table of Contents

Introduction

What you are holding is a book about Leica M-series cameras, yet it doesn't go into detail on the various camera types, models, and functions. This is pretty unusual!

The aim of this book is to communicate to you, the reader, the endless fun I have had during more than 30 years of shooting with Leica M cameras, and to help you find the same joy and satisfaction using your Leicas.

I have used many models over the years: I began with an M2 then switched to an M3. I initially skipped over the M4 and worked with the M6 for while before backtracking and acquiring an M4 as a backup body. I tried the M7, loved the MP, tested the Digital M8, and now shoot using an M9 and the M (Typ 240). If you are technically minded, you are probably thinking these cameras are not really comparable: some are analog, some digital; some have a built-in exposure meter while others don't; and they even include a mix of APS-H and full-frame sensors. A debate about the relative merits of all these features could fill many an evening.

But this book is about the technical features these cameras share, and most of all about the effect these features have on the photos they produce. Nearly all the lenses Leica has ever produced fit all the bodies listed above. All these bodies have a complex base plate that provides access to the camera's recording medium; and they are all mirrorless, about the same size, and can be used with Leica's Bright-line viewfinders. This last item is what makes a Leica so special. One could argue whether using such an optical/mechanical masterpiece makes sense in the digital age. After all, every Micro Four

Thirds camera has an electronic viewfinder that displays 100 percent of the image area so you don't have to guess how the framing will look in the image you capture. The Leica M system now offers a separate electronic viewfinder, although this makes virtually no difference to this book's central message.

As a professional photojournalist and documentary photographer, I work with whichever tools are necessary to fulfill my clients' wishes. I use DSLRs and multi-megapixel cameras whenever the job or the client demands it. I use super-wide-angle lenses, ultra-long telephotos, macro lenses, and flash.

It is the aspects of photography that are close to my heart that I want to talk about. No, I don't mean flower or landscape photography—I am talking about the aspects of photography that deal with people, which allows me to enter different worlds.

But let me begin by telling you about myself. I was given my first camera on my twelfth birthday. I was terribly disappointed because I really wanted a sports watch like the ones all my classmates had at the time. In addition to the camera, I was also given a book on photojournalism that, after an initial period of disdain, actually provided me with inspiration for many years to come. As my interest in photography grew, I acquired new cameras, practiced in my darkroom, started a photo club at school, and, in my free time, began to take photos for a local daily newspaper. My interest in photography varied up to the time I finished school and began studying medicine. To finance the soft-top VW Beetle that I so desperately needed to continue my studies, I began a side project I called "paid photojournalism." I devoured many books, newspaper articles, and magazines on the subject, and I shot endless numbers of photos. Never having formally studied photography, I learned everything I know from studying the media, reading countless books, and visiting many, many exhibitions. I now also use the opportunities presented by the Internet to study images and documentary coverage of all kinds of events. I have never been particularly attracted by big names. Rather, my guiding light has always simply been the images that I like. I only found out later which of these were created by masters of the genre.

I was fortunate enough to turn my hobby into my profession and that is still the case today. The main thrust of my professional work is more corporate than journalistic, but my great love remains photographing people with my Leica—an aspect of my work that I incorporate in commercial projects as often as possible.

Throughout this book I use interesting and unique images as examples that will teach you to enjoy your photography and your Leica more than ever. I will show you ways to become one with your camera and how to shoot photos that will excite and interest other people. I want to encourage you to leave behind familiar ways of working and to follow new paths.

You may ask what this introduction has to do with a book about Leicas and whether the ideas I present would be as valid for any camera. My answer is a resounding "No." Working with a Leica, especially in this day and age, represents a unique approach to photography. Shooting with a Leica slows you down and demands your full attention at every stage of the image creation process. This is a challenge that has its own rewards.

I bought my first Leica—a battered M2 with a standard lens—when I was 16. That was the camera that taught me photography and how to survive with a single fixed-focal-length lens. I used it to practice composition and it gave me the excuse I needed to be inquisitive. But it was a touchy camera, too and if it didn't like the way I approached my work, it produced bad photos. In short, that camera was my earliest photographic mentor. During my entire career, it has always been my Leicas that demand humility, accuracy, and equanimity from me, and in turn have enabled me to continue to climb the ladder to photographic success.

I invite you to break the rules, take chances, and get creative. The end result is what matters, regardless of whether your image was captured using analog, digital, or hybrid technology.

Bertram Solcher

Hamburg, September 2014

1. The Invisible Photographer
Clothing and Behavior

In my introduction, I promised you a photo book that takes an unusual approach, which is why this chapter is not about multi-pocket vests and jackets, off-road shoes, all-weather hats, or photo bags. In my opinion, specialized photo clothing only benefits the person selling it.

Why am I so adamant about this? Simply because this book is about photographing people in their normal, everyday surroundings. Imagine the following scenario with two very different photographers setting out to capture images at a flea market:

Photographer #1 dresses in a comfortable pair of red pants with big pockets from a safari equipment supplier, adds a pair of neon green sneakers (the kind that enable you to fly through the streets), and completes his outfit with a khaki-colored photo vest with a film manufacturer's logo on it. He then grabs his largest camera bag (you never know what you are going to need), shoulders his tripod with its hydraulic tilt/swivel head, hangs a DSLR with a telephoto zoom around his neck, and pulls on his Yankees cap. Anyone who sees him on location will probably assume he is either some kind of strange cargo-laden parrot or simply insane. Neither will help him with the job at hand.

Photographer #2 dresses in jeans, comfortable everyday shoes, and an inconspicuous jacket with a couple of pockets in which he puts a spare battery, a memory card (or film), and a spare lens. He carries his Leica over his shoulder and most people will assume he is just another casual market visitor. His photographic intentions are not immediately obvious.

Meanwhile, simply getting to the location carrying all that gear has taken its toll and our "parrot" needs a drink. While taking a break, he suddenly spots a potential victim: an aging antiques dealer. He has seen on TV how photographers chase stars, so he sets off at a run. Unfortunately, his tripod slips off his shoulder, landing on the ground with a crash and ensuring that everyone is now looking his way. While bending down to pick it up, his camera bag slips off other shoulder and, in an attempt to rescue it, he knocks his cap off and sends it flying into the drinks in the booth where he had been resting. At this point he loses his nerve and decides to go home and take some comparison test shots for his favorite DSLR forum instead.

Photographer #2, our Leica man, has also spotted the antiques dealer. He walks calmly up to the seller's booth, slowly raises the camera, focuses calmly, and releases the shutter. Maybe the dealer has spotted him, but the calm concentration he radiates communicates no sense of disquiet. Maybe the antiques man gave the photographer his permission with a slight smile or maybe he asked what the photos were for—we don't really know.

You might find this comparison an exaggeration, but there are more characters like our photographer #1 on the prowl than you might think. Even pro photographers often give too little thought to what they wear, the gear they take along, and how they behave with their subjects. When I am out and about, I often hear remarks like, "Have you taken any photos yet? Really? I didn't notice."

I try to blend in with the environment and adapt my movements appropriately. I dress and behave as inconspicuously as possible and don't use large photo bags or huge lenses. And a Leica, of course, is small, quiet, and unobtrusive. An M-series camera doesn't look like most people's idea of a pro-grade photographic tool and, as a result, Leica users are often greeted with a friendly smile or even amusement and make comments like, "I didn't know you could still take photos with such an old camera." Consider how you would feel as a subject if you were approached by someone holding a huge DSLR with an even larger lens attached. Like most people, you would probably feel threatened if confronted with someone whose face is almost completely obscured by a large black machine with a huge protrusion on its front.

Apart from one eye, a Leica user's face is almost completely visible and his facial expression is identifiable and therefore not off-putting. You see? Great photography, and Leica M photography especially, requires more than just knowing how to operate a camera.

I have made it my guiding motto to take photos of others as I would have others take photos of my family or me. This doesn't mean that I don't create humorous images; I just avoid embarrassing my subjects. I am quite capable of having a laugh about a funny photo of myself.

Many documentary photographers use military-sounding terms such as aiming and shooting to describe how they work. When asked about his technique, Henri Cartier-Bresson, one of the founders of the legendary Magnum photo agency, summarized his approach thus: "Aim well, shoot fast, and scram." There are situations in which I prefer to remain invisible and unrecognized, but I don't like to "steal" an image of a subject. I appreciate positive reactions and enjoy making contact with people. Peter Turnley, an American photographer living in Paris, works in a similar way. If you check out his Facebook page, his website, or one of his fantastic Parisian photo books, you will see that taking photos can be just as much about making friends as capturing images.

To get back to the real subject of this chapter, have you ever considered how attractive a Leica can be? Yes, get out and "wear" your Leica! A Leica doesn't like being kept in a cabinet or at the bottom of a photo bag. It enjoys being slung over your shoulder or carried, perhaps lightly covered, on your chest. A Leica likes to be switched on, primed with a useful combination of aperture and shutter speed, and taken out for a walk in the fresh air. Have you ever asked yourself how many photographic opportunities you have missed because your camera was buried in the depths of your bag or, worse still, you didn't even have it with you? OK, so you will now take your camera with you wherever you go. Promise? Or maybe you have promised yourself that you will take at least one picture per day. It will be great practice if you do.

Which brings me to this chapter's lesson. Did I already explain about the lessons? At the end of each chapter you will find a practical exercise that will help you to put the theory covered by the text into practice.

Photo Exercise #1

What you need: Your Leica, a lens (28mm, 35mm, or 50mm), film/memory card

Take your camera and head off to a location of your choice such as a railroad station, a flea market, a busy pedestrian crossing, or a street party. Look for a person or situation that you would like to photograph, raise your camera slowly and calmly to your eye, focus and release the shutter smoothly but positively. Now lower your camera just as calmly. Try to develop a fluid rhythm with no sudden movements. Were you close enough to your subject? If not, get closer. Then get closer still. If you do everything right, hardly anyone will notice you are taking pictures.

The second step in this exercise is to repeat the first step, but this time make eye contact with your subjects and thus obtain permission to shoot. And remember, unspoken permission counts, too.

The Soccer World Cup

What could I photograph to capture the spirit of the World Cup? In Brazil, at the playing venue, there would have been countless opportunities, but what about at home in Germany?

I have to admit, I'm not a big soccer fan, and what I like most about the game is the feeling of community it generates. I like to go to a bar and watch a game on TV, but the game is always less important than watching the people around me. The emotional outbursts from the "barroom coaches" can be extremely funny (even if they are not always politically correct). And if I miss an important play, I can always watch the replays.

During the 2014 tournament, I went to the local sports bar with my wife and daughter, and I took along my M9 and Typ 240 bodies with 50mm and 28mm lenses. My approach was to order a beer with my camera clearly visible before I began to photograph the people around me.

In Germany, public soccer viewings take place in the open, so I was able to move around without any fuss. I began by taking a few snaps of my wife and daughter before branching out to include strangers. Initially, I often had to explain what I was doing. Most people don't mind being photographed but may be concerned that their images will be published on the Internet without their consent.

I always ask my subjects for permission to publish, whether on social networks or elsewhere, and I always give my subjects my card so they can get in touch and give me a mailing address where I can send images, as a kind of payment. Anyway, what was I going to photograph? I had planned to document the tournament without featuring the game itself, and I wanted to capture the spirit of the event by way of gestures and the interactions among the people watching the game.

I neglected to consider that most of the matches would be broadcast in the evening, and I was already set on not using flash. This meant I had to shoot with very little ambient light, so I used ISO settings between 1600 and 3200 coupled with the maximum available aperture and exposure times of 1/30 or 1/60. Surprisingly, I ended up with very few blurred images. Sure, there was some motion blur involved, but that was mostly deliberate and it contributed to the mood of my images. At high ISO values, my Typ 240 had no problem with the minimal available light, and I only had to perform slight adjustments later in Lightroom. In the end, I was really excited by the number of pin-sharp images I managed to capture by focusing on my subjects' eyes—an approach that is easy to master using these cameras, even in very poor light. If a person's eyes are not sharp in the resulting image, it can only be due to sloppy focusing, or unplanned movement on the part of the photographer or the subject. If an entire image was blurred, it is usually because I moved the camera during the exposure.

Take a look at the images and decide for yourself whether I managed to capture an unusual World Cup mood away from the usual hubbub.

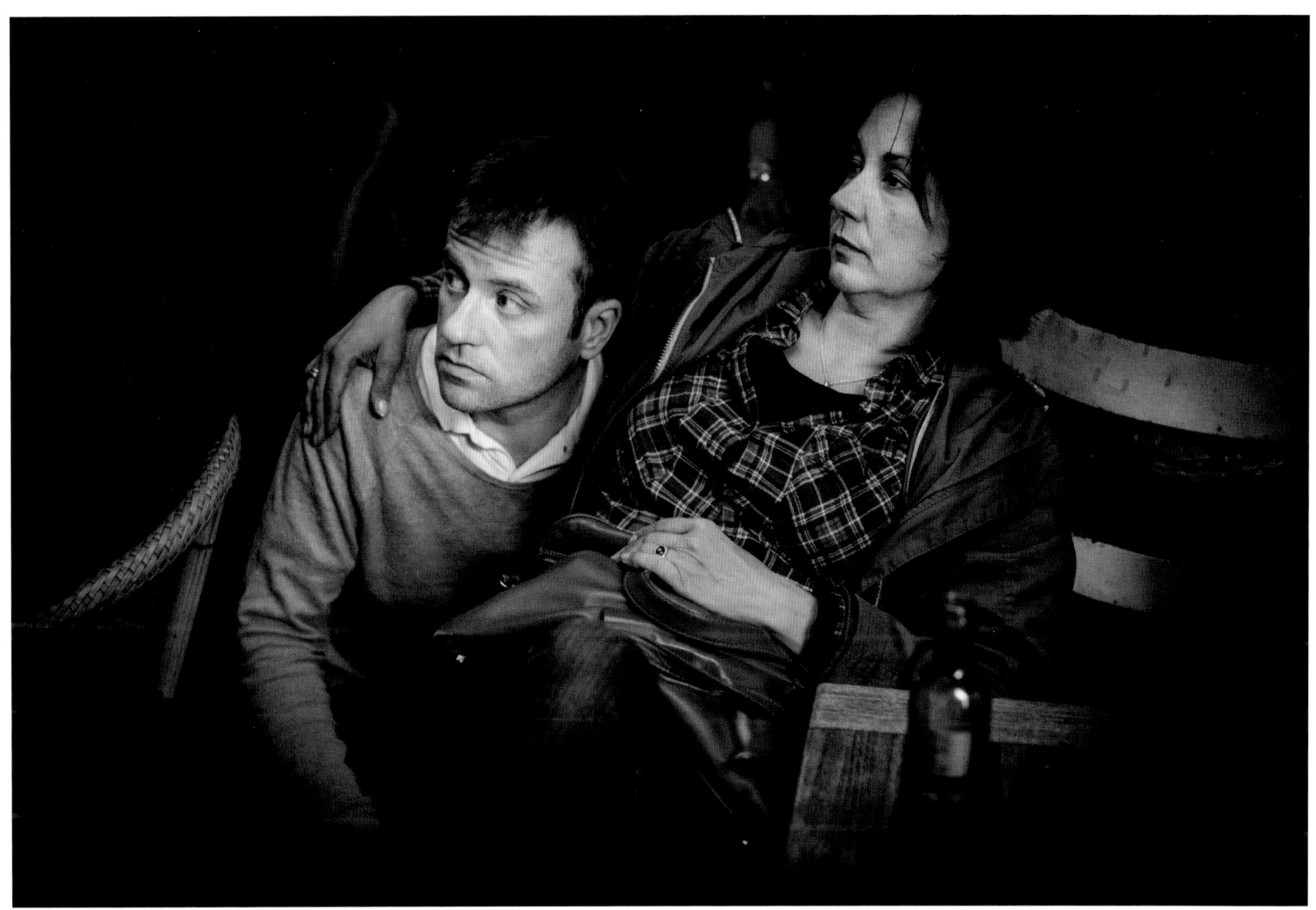

The events on the screen are much more important than the presence of the camera

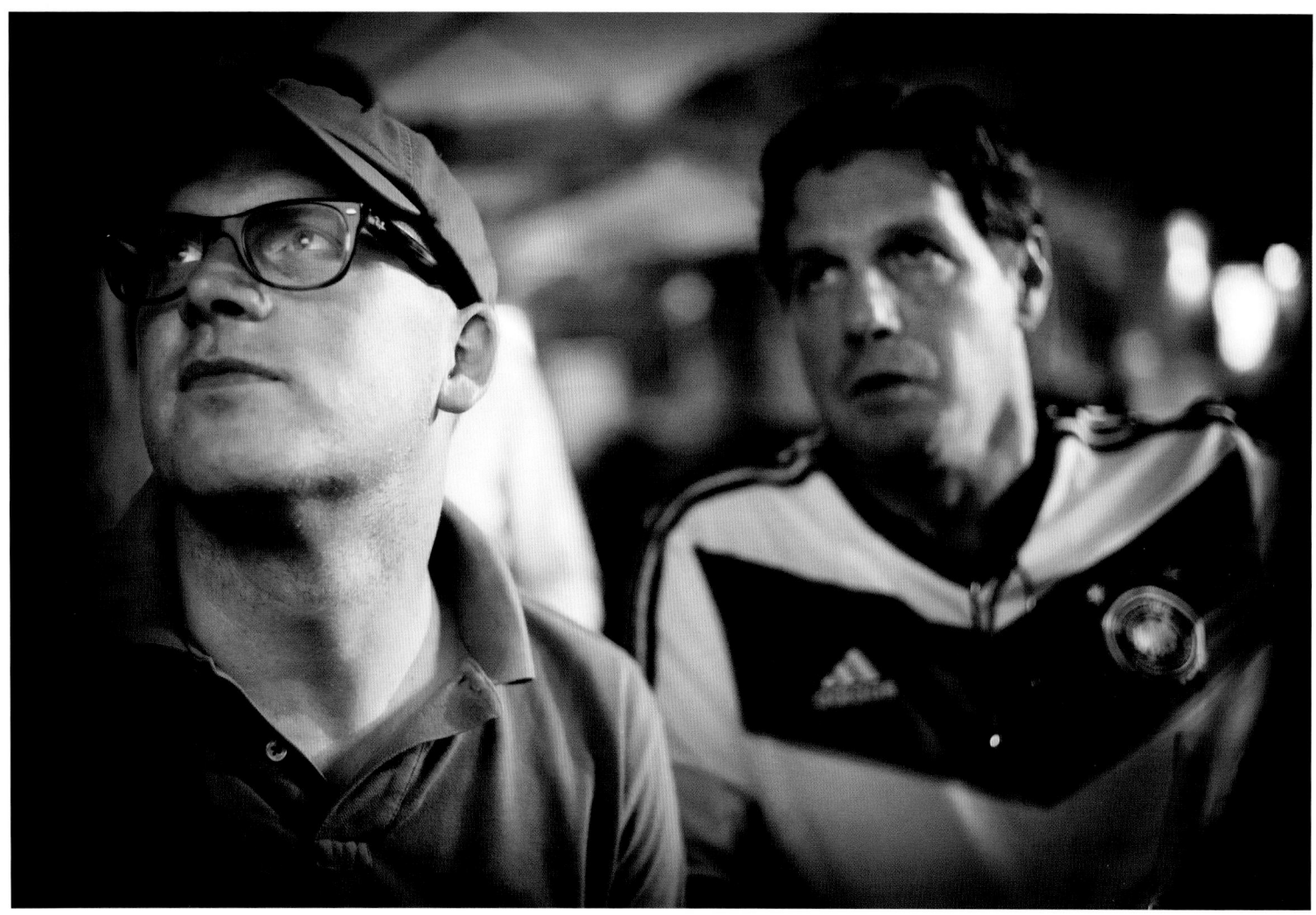
All eyes on the screen. The tension is palpable.

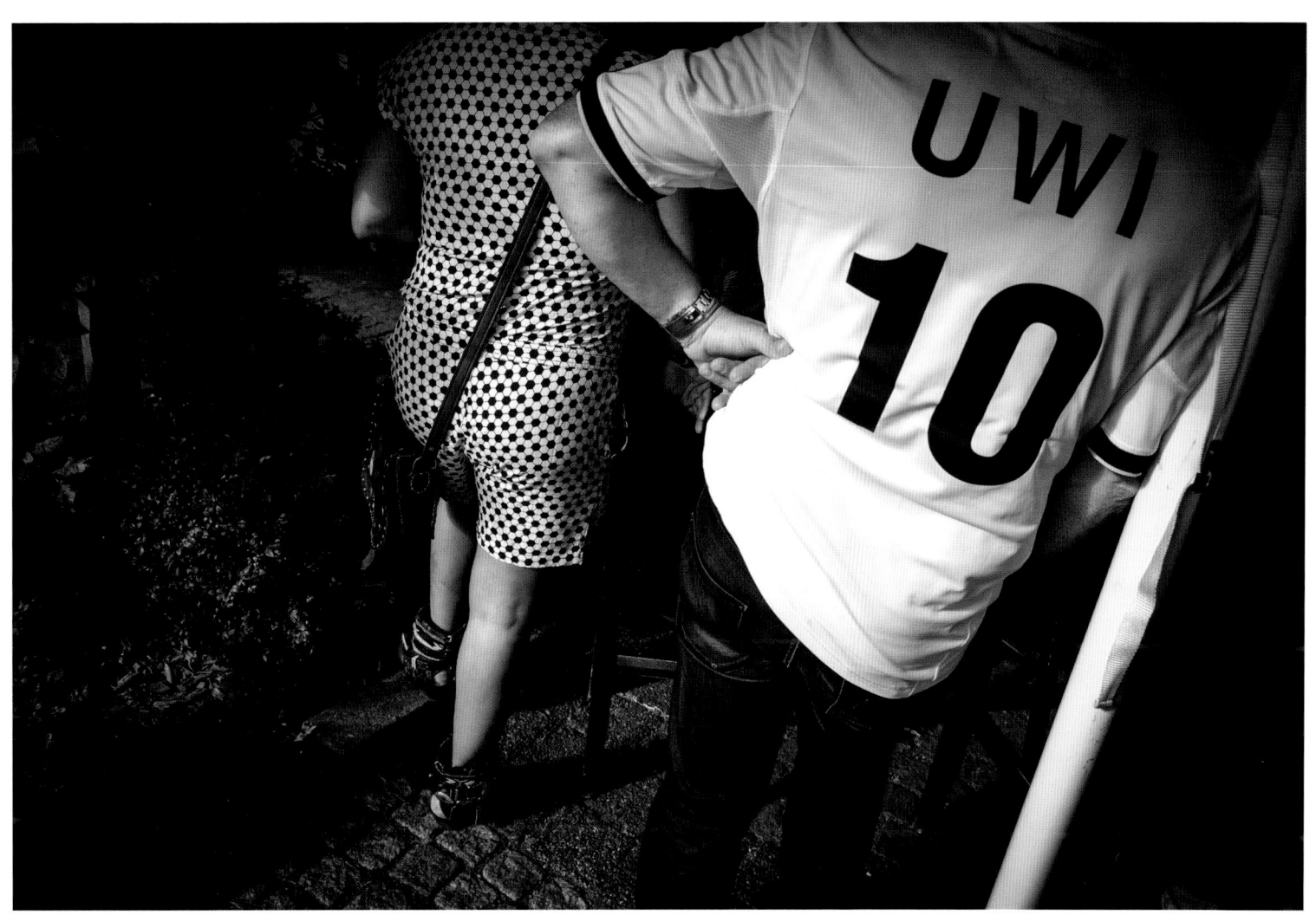

An equal rights outfit. One pattern fits all!

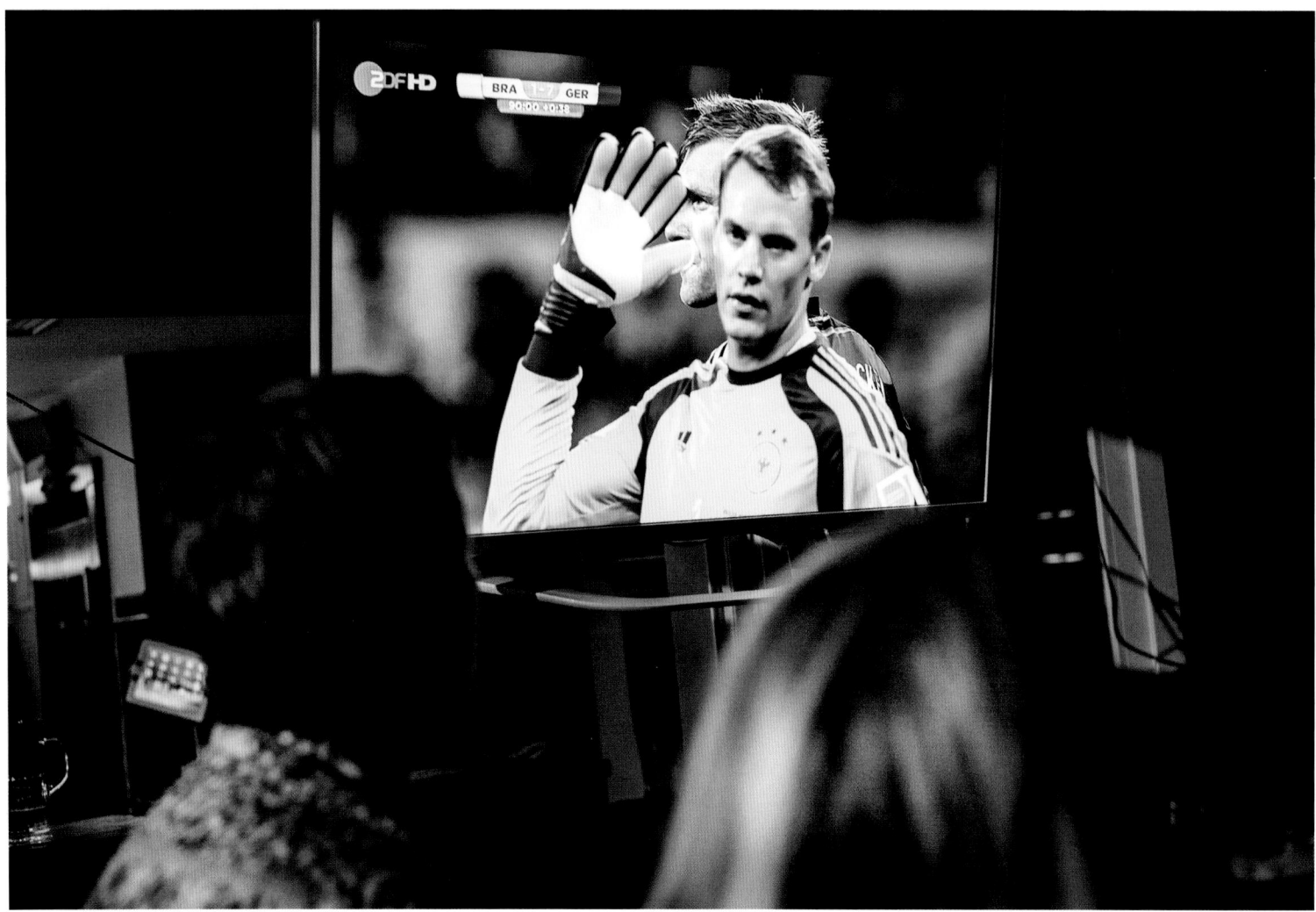

Sometimes the players talk to their fans directly through the screen

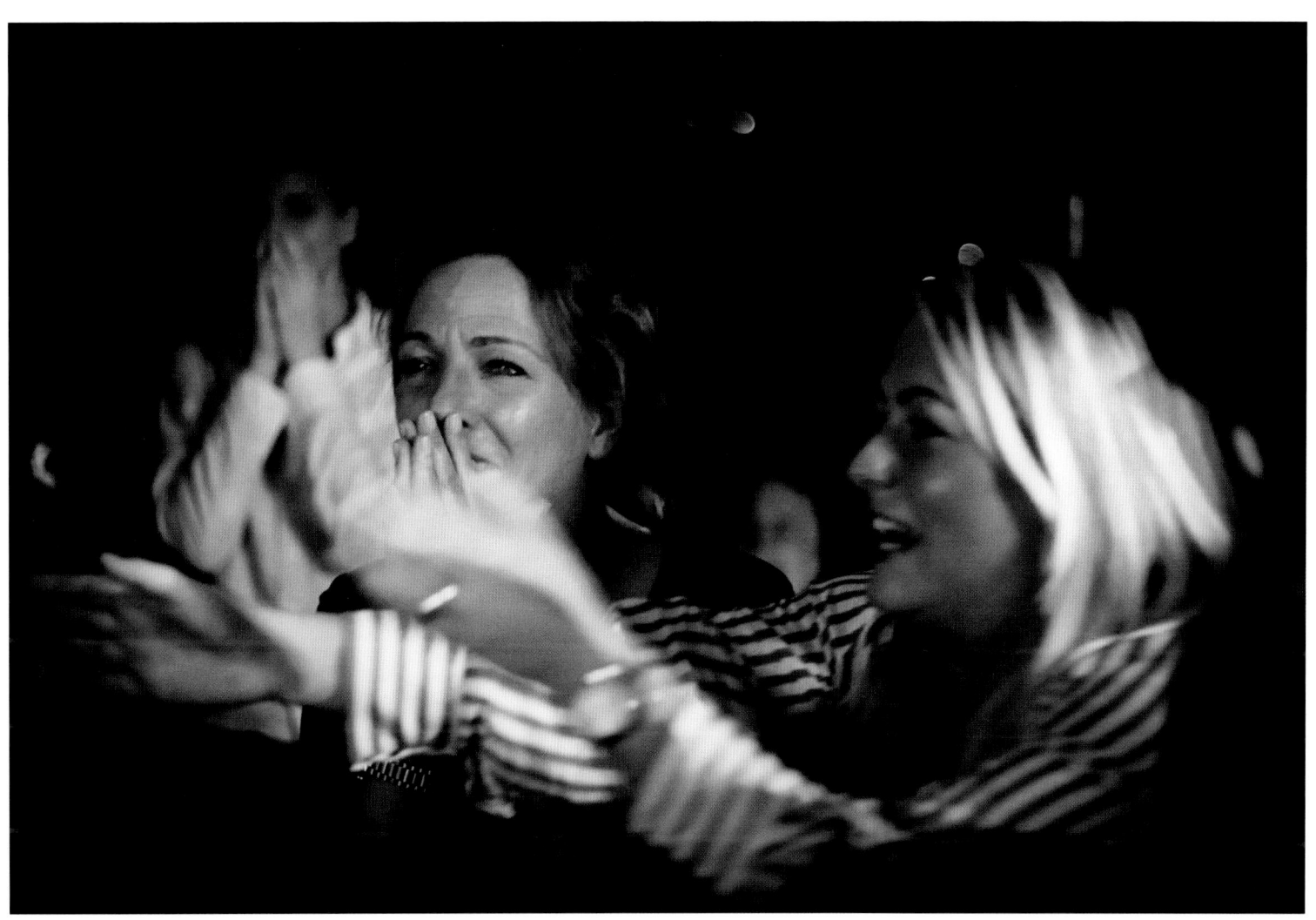

Joy and wonder during the Germany vs. Brazil game (Germany won 7-1)

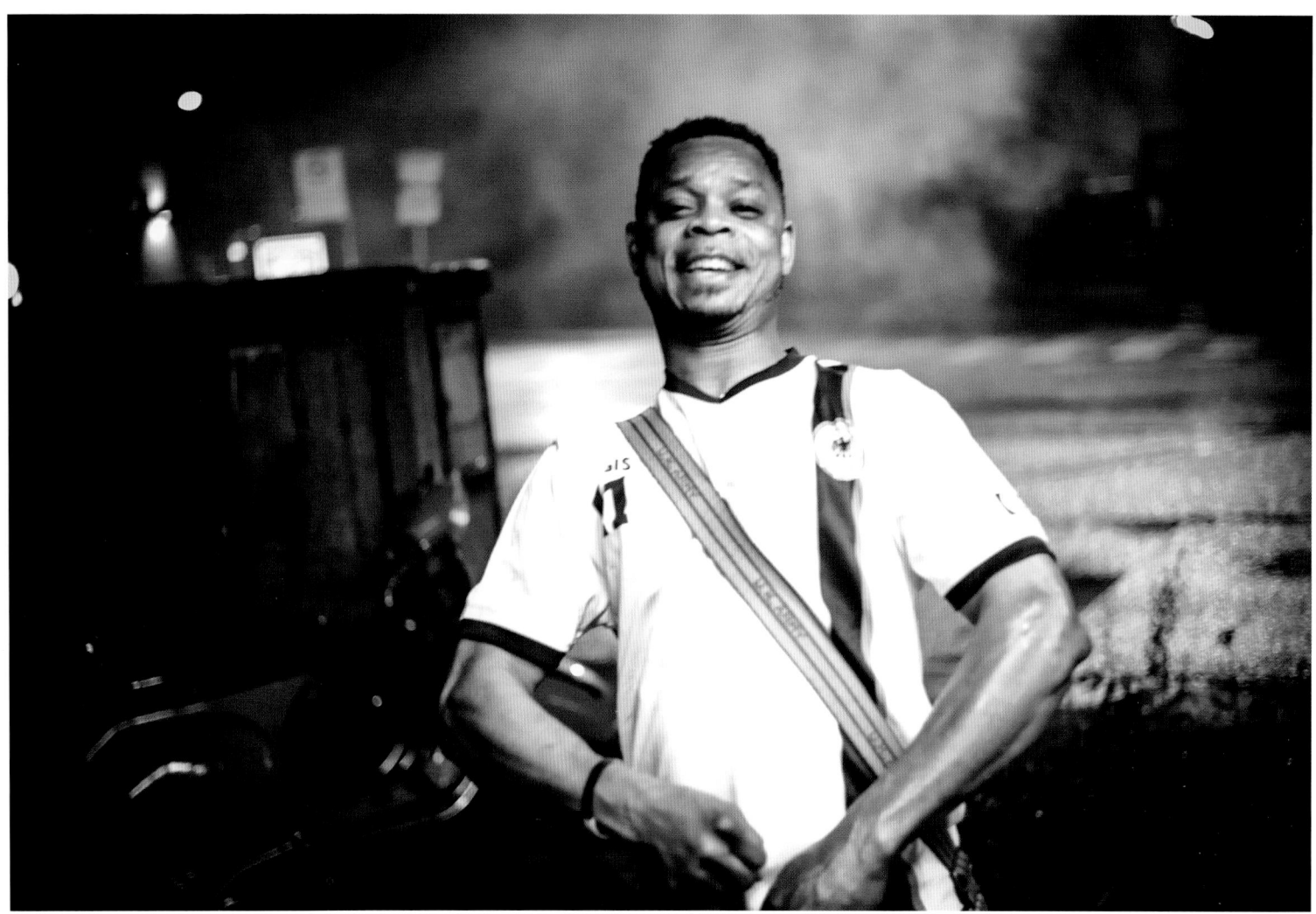

This guy insisted on having his photo taken, and the slight motion blur adds authenticity

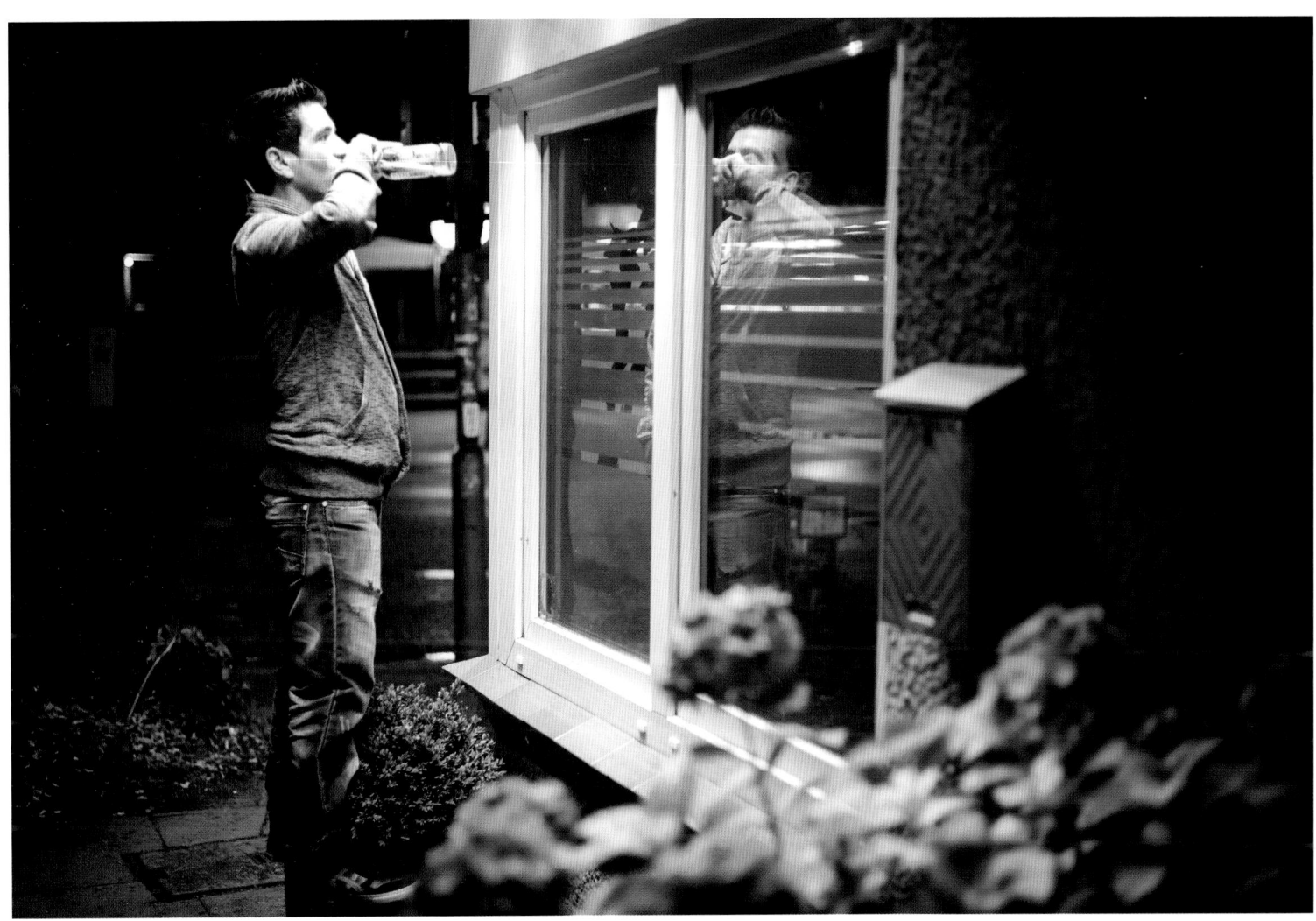

The weather was bad during the final and dry seats were rare. The reflections in the window increase the tension.

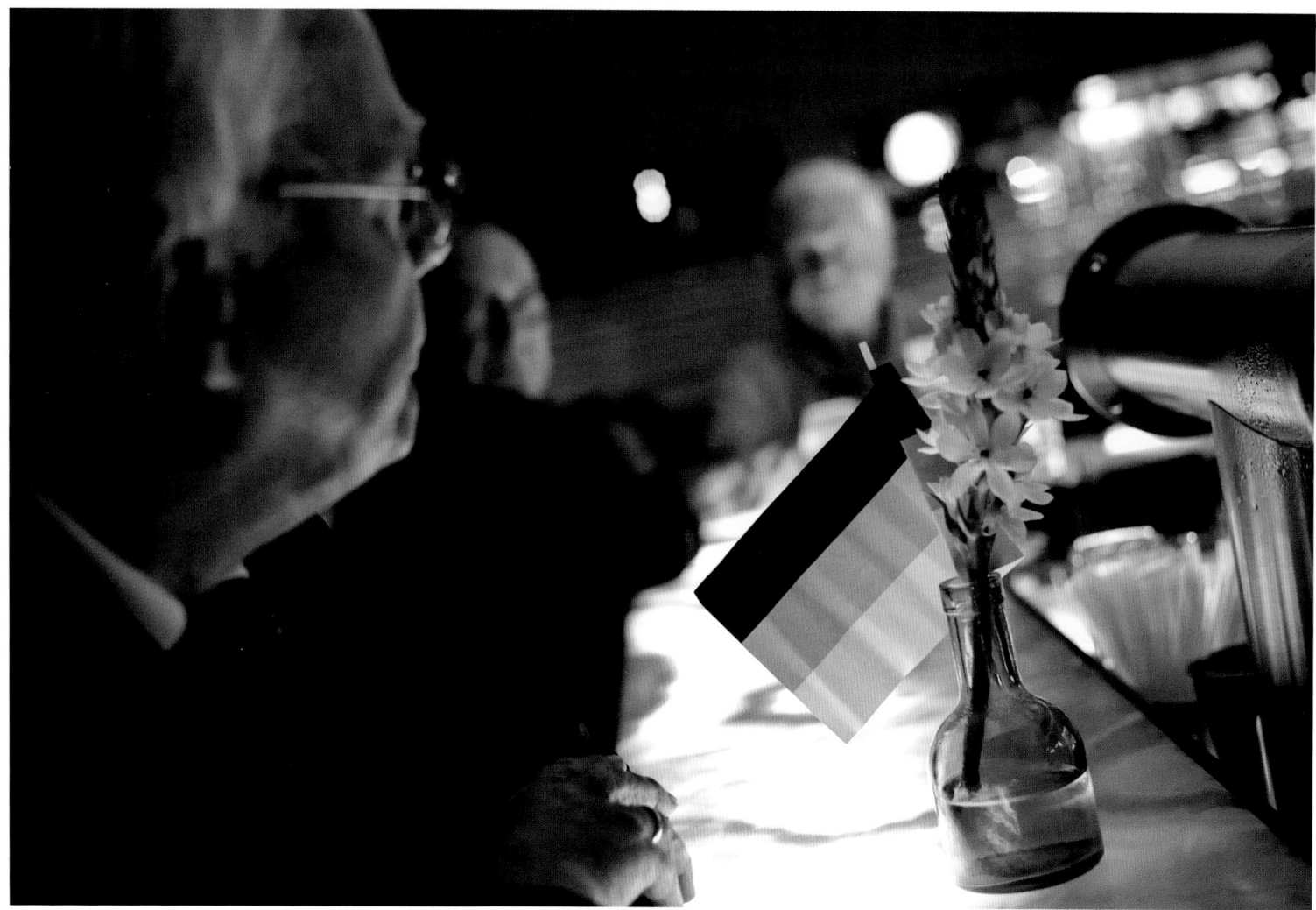

A still life to round out the sequence

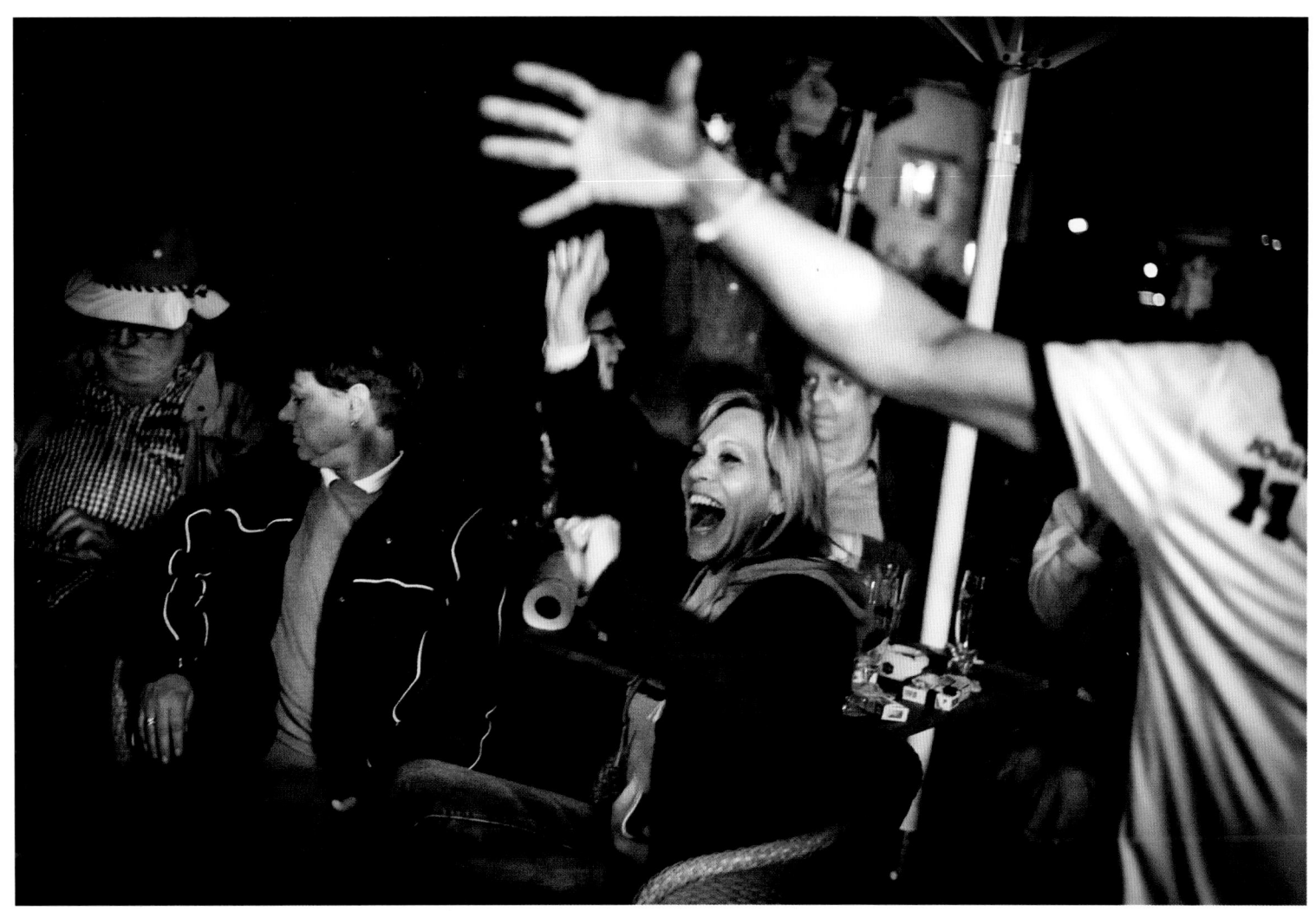

World champions?

2. Less is More
Selecting Your Gear

Now that we have talked about the importance of your demeanor, I want to help you see your equipment in a different light. In photographic circles, the question of what gear to use is hotly debated, so let's be clear about it from the start: There is no right or wrong gear! A photo captured using an iPhone can get printed on the cover of Time magazine, while other photos captured using the most expensive gear can be best described as visual pollution.

I have always been curious to hear and read about the gear used by established photographers, and I have often followed suit and purchased some of the items they mention. However, I have never been able to duplicate the images that impressed me just by using the same equipment. Familiarity with the gear is essential and there are certain things you need to perform specific tasks—for example, sports photographers simply must use telephoto lenses; and you can't do without a macro lens if you want to shoot extreme close-ups.

Digital or Analog

So what is the best way to approach the Leica system? The first question you have to answer is, digital or analog? In principle, the only real difference between the two is the type of storage medium they use, and this makes no discernible difference to the image-capture process. You have to admit that it makes no difference whether you save images on a SanDisk or a Lexar memory card and, by the same token, it doesn't matter if you store your images on film or digital media. Images captured by these two very different methods may have distinctive appearances, but images captured using different types of film have their own look too, and images captured using different digital cameras look different as well. Our overarching aim, however, is not to store images but to present them, and I will go into more detail on that particular subject later on.

I can almost hear cries from the analog community telling me that digital image capture can never be classified as true photography—primarily because images captured digitally can be duplicated at will. This may be true, but a great image doesn't care whether it was captured digitally or using an analog process. This book is all about images and what they represent, not about esoteric questions of brand loyalty or the effectiveness of marketing strategies. In all the chapters that follow, I will not be differentiating between digital and analog Leicas.

Choose a Lens—or Better Yet, Use Your Feet

Once you have decided which camera body to use, you need a lens to go with it. This, too, is a hot topic. Personally, I hate the endless conversations that take place between seasoned aficionados, so let's just keep to the facts.

Leica markets standard, wide-angle, super-wide-angle, and telephoto lenses. Budget permitting, the lenses within these groups cover just about any photographic task you can imagine—and this is where the "less-is-more" approach comes in.

My DSLR camera bag contains lenses with focal lengths between 14mm and 200mm, a macro lens, various teleconverters, and a bunch of other bits and pieces that add up to a total of almost 30l pounds of metal and glass. My Leica bag, on the other hand, usually contains just one body and two lenses. You are probably wondering how I can achieve the results I am looking for using so little gear. I don't claim to be able to cover the same ground with my Leica that I can with my DSLR, and I will continue to mistreat my neck and back doing the jobs that require heavy lifting.

I don't use my Leica to capture close-ups or long telephoto shots, and only rarely do I use it with flash.

So when do I use my Leica? The quick answer is, in any situation in which I can freely select my shooting position. Joining a group of professional sports photographers squeezed into a dugout with their huge telephotos lenses is definitely not a "Leica moment."

If we can move around freely, any limitations to how we shoot are of a completely different nature and have primarily to do with our fear of being too conspicuous or of getting too close to strangers. In these kinds of situations, using your feet is the best way to change your viewpoint. Two steps forward or back can make the difference between wide-angle and normal perspectives; the same is true for the switch between normal and short telephoto.

Now that I've got you moving, I nevertheless have to ruin your dream of a one-lens kit. Every lens has strengths and it would be a shame not to have two or three different choices on hand.

I am not about to present the ultimate solution to all of your questions about what to take with you and what to leave at home. First of all, you need to consider what you as a human being bring to the party. In other words, I want to talk about your eyes.

The Focal Length and Depth of Field of the Human Eye

What do you think is the focal length of your eyes? The human eye has a very similar angle of view and perspective to that of a 50mm lens, and the only Leica exception to this rule is the M8 with its crop-format APS-H sensor. This means that a 50mm lens "sees" the distances between objects just like we do. A wide-angle lens increases apparent distances; the shorter its focal length, the more pronounced the effect. The opposite is true of telephoto lenses that compress distances; and the greater the focal length, the closer distant objects appear to one another. Lenses can deceive the eye, and that is an important factor in the process of image composition. We also assume that we can see everything from the near foreground to the farthest background in focus. Unfortunately, real-world experience teaches us otherwise—especially when we hit 40 years of age and we realize that it takes a little longer than it used to switch focus from a page in a book to the view outside the window. Because our eyes instinctively focus on the middle distance, we think we see everything in focus. Like our eyes, camera lenses have a limited depth of focus, which is why they have a focus ring in the first place. All Leica lenses have a depth-of-field scale engraved beside the focus scale and, if you take a close look at it, you will discover that depth of field is very shallow at large apertures and deeper at smaller apertures. To add to the confusion, the shorter the focal length of a lens, the greater the depth of focus for a constant aperture setting.

Let's look at an example: for a 50mm lens set to f/16, the depth of focus ranges from about 2.4 meters to infinity, whereas the field of focus for a 35mm lens set to f/16 begins at a distance of about 1.2 meters. Finally, you need to know that the closer you get to the subject, the smaller the field of focus will become.

To summarize:

- Long focal length = shallow depth of field; short focal length = greater depth of field.
- Large aperture = shallow depth of field; small aperture = greater depth of field
- Close subject = shallow depth of field; distant subject = greater depth of field (dependent also on the focal length of the lens)

Focal Lengths and Angles of View

We haven't yet discussed the differences between the angles of view produced by short (wide-angle) and long (telephoto) focal lengths. In this respect, human vision and the visual data captured by camera lenses differ significantly. If you let your eye wander from one side of a room to the other, your brain creates the illusion of viewing a wide-angle image, although what we actually see is a series of "standard" 50mm images arranged in sequence to form a kind of virtual panorama. Remember, a 50mm lens captures an angle of view and perspective just like that perceived by the human eye.

If I want to capture an image of the same room in a single shot using my Leica, I would have to use a wide-angle lens, which would then produce an image with a very different look and feel from my human view. Because a wide-angle lens makes objects appear farther apart than they actually are, the resulting image makes the room seem larger than it really is. Before I delve into what is inside my camera bag, we need to look at one other aspect of the difference between human and camera vision. Most humans are able to see in three dimensions, whereas a camera can only record two. Because a camera cannot "see" in three dimensions, other aspects of the image capture process take on increased significance.

Photographic compositions often use the relative distances between objects to contribute to the feeling of depth in an image, and this is where the quality of lens optics comes into play. Leica M-series lenses have their own special way of portraying physical depth. They distinguish very clearly between the sharp and blurred portions of the field of focus, enabling us to precisely control the degree of background blur, thus enhancing the three-dimensional appearance of a photo. This high-quality background blur—also known as bokeh—is one of the most important compositional tools available to Leica photographers. I am telling you all this to encourage you to actively select your lenses and utilize the compositional control they provide.

What's in My Bag?

So, what wonderful things actually find their way into my Leica bag? I usually carry my 35mm and 50mm f/2.0 Summicrons, if necessary a 28mm or 24mm lens, and sometimes a 75mm as well. The reason I use this modest setup is because I like to shoot densely packed images from quite close up. Because most of my subjects are people who don't like having their personal space invaded, I rarely use wide-angle lenses. My 50mm is my favorite Leica lens. It shows life the way it is and all I have to do is construct an image around the events at hand. I also like using my 75mm because of its obvious telephoto effect, but also because the frame it produces in the viewfinder is still large enough to focus accurately.

In addition to a body and lenses, I carry spare memory cards for my M9 and my Typ 240, a piece of white plastic for making manual white balance settings, microfiber cleaning cloths, and a tabletop tripod that I can also use as a chest support if necessary. I also take along a pencil or a roller ball pen (these usually work in cold and the wet weather) and a notebook. I have a number of small, inconspicuous bags that don't look like camera bags, and I often take just a camera and a single lens with me, and I carry a spare battery and a few memory cards in my pocket.

Even if you own several lenses, try going out on a shoot with just one. You will be amazed how inspiring such a voluntary limitation can be.

Photo Exercise #2

What you need: Your Leica, a 35mm or 50mm lens, film or memory card, insulating tape

Use the tape to fix the focus ring of your lens at a distance of about 1.5 meters and use the aperture to control focus, always remembering to adjust the exposure time to suit your settings. I know this is a challenging way to shoot, but that's the point: It's a great way to learn about your own capabilities and those of your camera.

Leica Customer Care

I have always been motivated by curiosity and wanted to find things out for myself. I discovered that my camera gave me access to people and places that are not accessible to everyone.

Leica as a company has interested me for years. I had been lucky enough to get first-hand experience of the camera-manufacturing process but until recently I didn't know what happens to a camera that has to be serviced or repaired. Usually I give my camera to a friendly person at a counter who asks me to come back in a few days and then he and my camera disappear through a door. This book gave me the perfect opportunity to take a look behind the scenes at Leica Customer Care.

Once I received permission to shoot, I drove the 280 miles from my home in Hamburg to Wetzlar in heavy fall rain—not the best shooting conditions. Leica's new head office lies on the outskirts of the small industrial town of Wetzlar and I had originally planned to include an outdoor shot of the building in my report. As I approached, I saw the building as a background to the raindrops on the windshield. I parked where I could see the whole complex in one broad sweep through the glass. I focused some of my shots on the raindrops and some on the building, and once again saw proof that any weather can be great weather for taking photos, as long as you go with the flow.

While I was shooting, the sun appeared from behind the clouds, the light changed completely, and, because it was still raining, a wonderful rainbow formed above the Leica building.

The new Leica head office building is home to Customer Care, company management, the Leica World exhibition space and gallery, and a Leica store. Visitors are also allowed to take a peek at the manufacturing process.

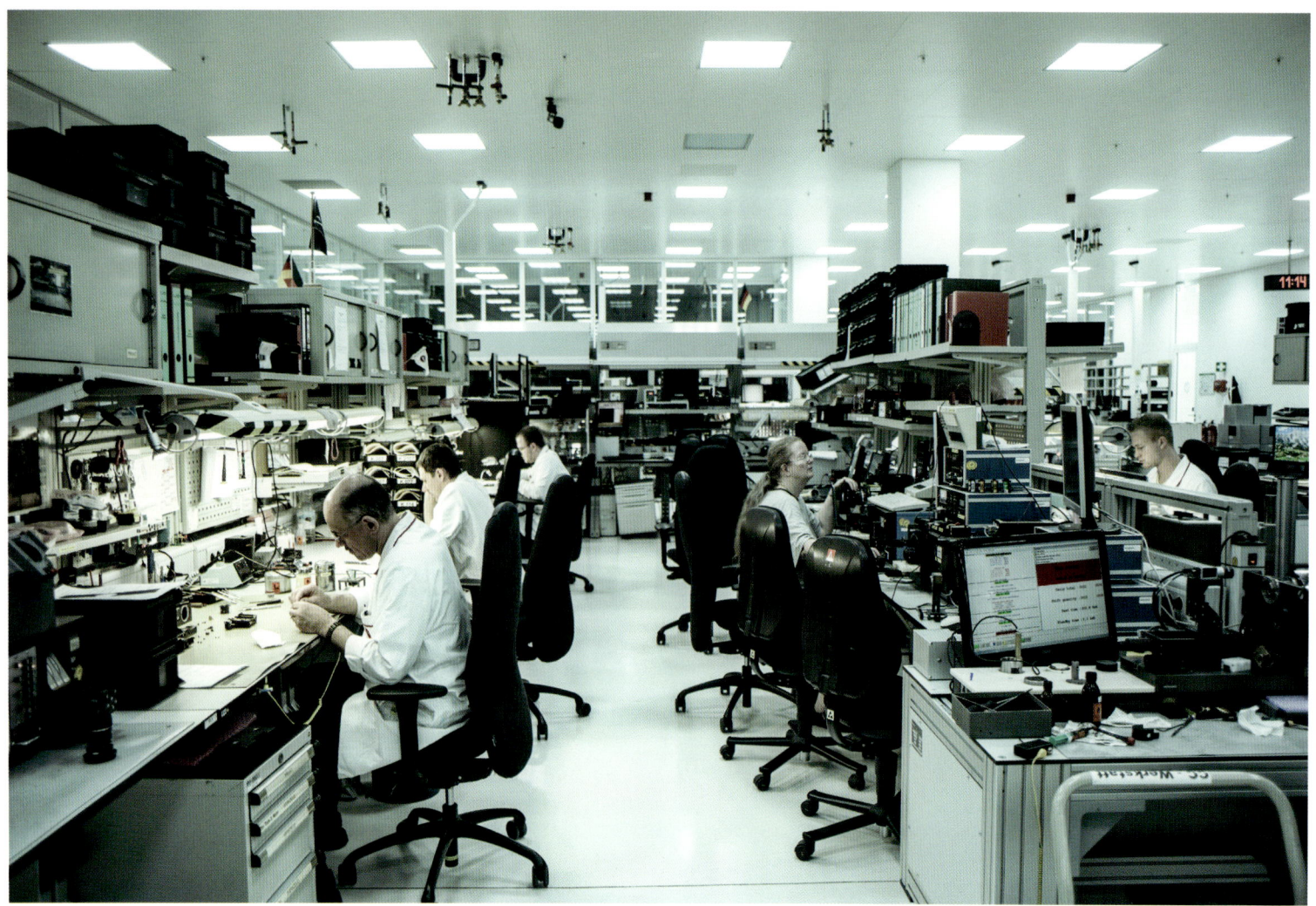

Part of the Leica M maintenance department

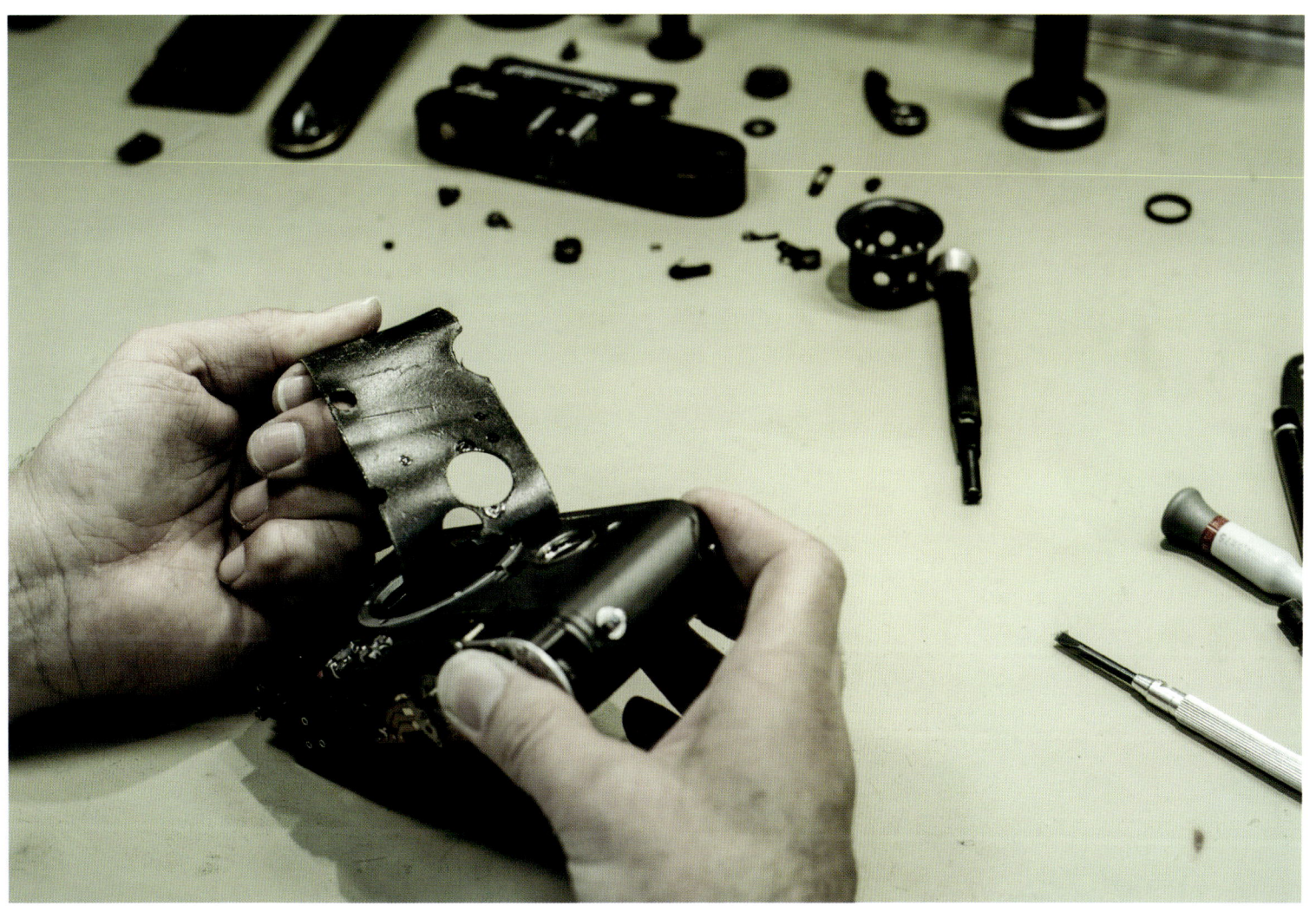

"Undressing" a Leica MP

If I had allowed myself to be put off by the weather, I would never have had the opportunity to capture that unusual architectural shot. The next day, I was taken into the inner sanctum of Leica Customer Care. I don't remember what I was expecting, but it definitely wasn't the view that awaited me. The sheer size of the department amazed me. I had underestimated the sense of responsibility to its customers that had been created in the 60 years of Leica M history. I had also overlooked the fact that Leica also manufactures binoculars, microscopes, and other precision optical instruments.

The most impressive part of the experience was being allowed to observe the love and care with which every camera was handled. I was allowed to photograph a member of the M group as he repaired a heavily used analog MP.

I had my standard M9, Typ 240, 28mm, 35mm and 50mm kit with me, which turned out not to be the best choice. The engineer who was working on the MP didn't just service it; he dismantled it completely before cleaning and lubricating its various moving parts and replacing worn-out components.

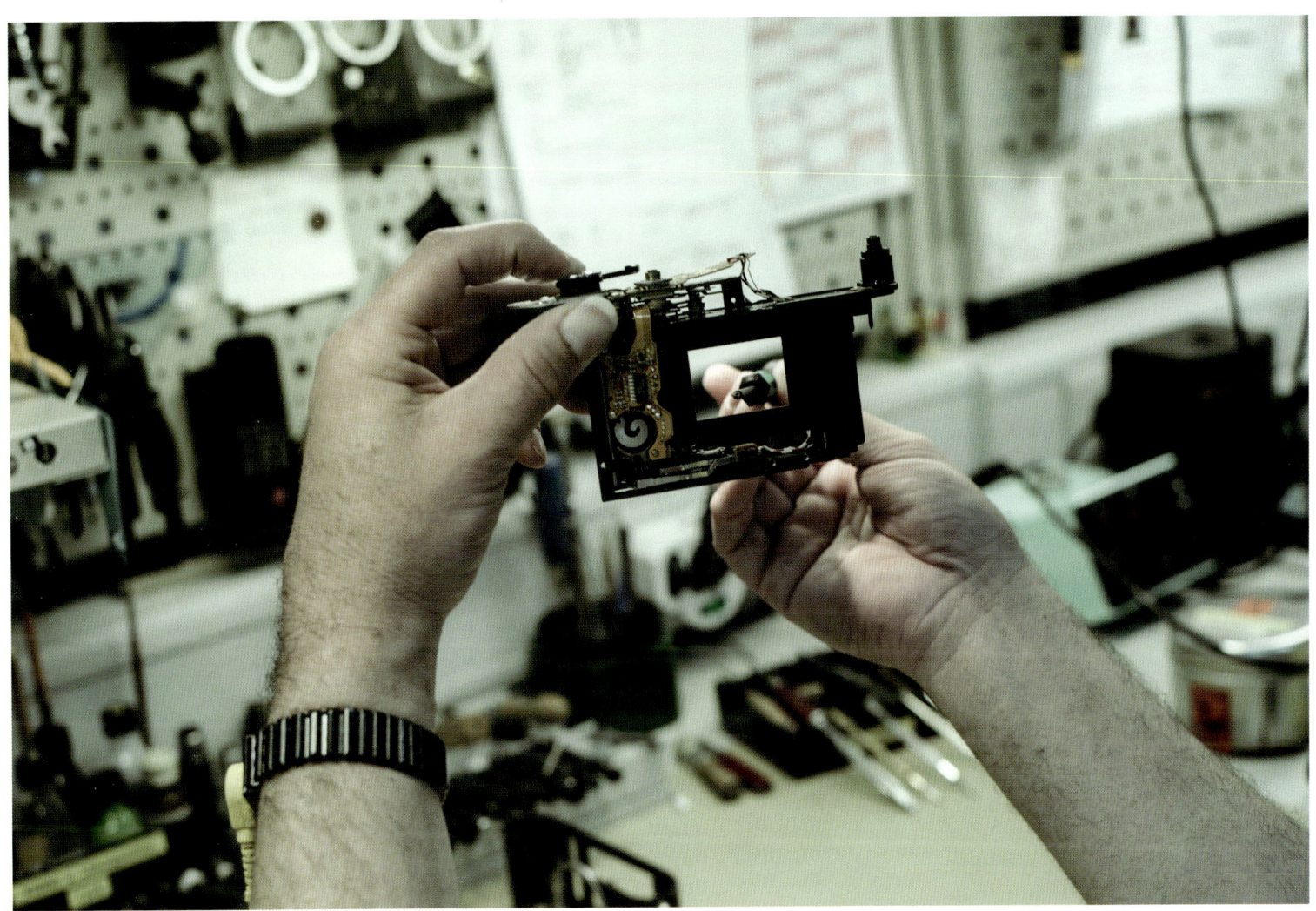

The shutter is nearly all that is left in one piece

A DSLR with a macro lens would have made my work easier; but that was out of the question. In the end, with a little extra effort, I was able to shoot good images of the small parts using my M, simply by including a little more of the surroundings in the images than I would have using a macro.

Watching the MP being taken apart almost caused me physical pain, especially when the engineer began to peel off the leather coating to gain access to the screws that hold together the core of the camera. Leica technicians are surrounded by cupboards and drawers filled with M-series camera parts. Digital and analog cameras undergo the same rigorous initial inspections, although digital Leicas are analyzed using many more computer-based tests than their analog counterparts.

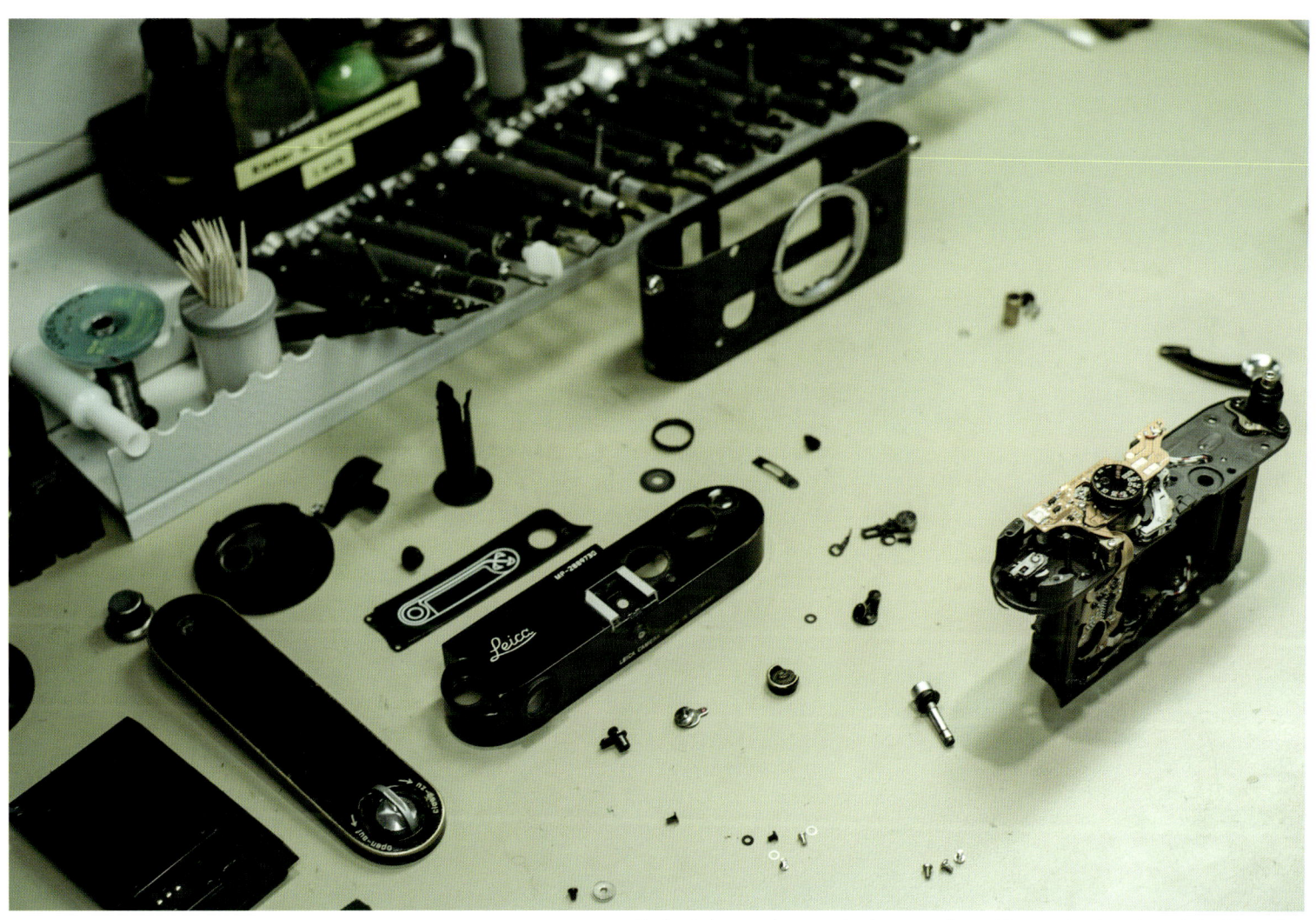

Order is key and every single screw found its way back to its original location

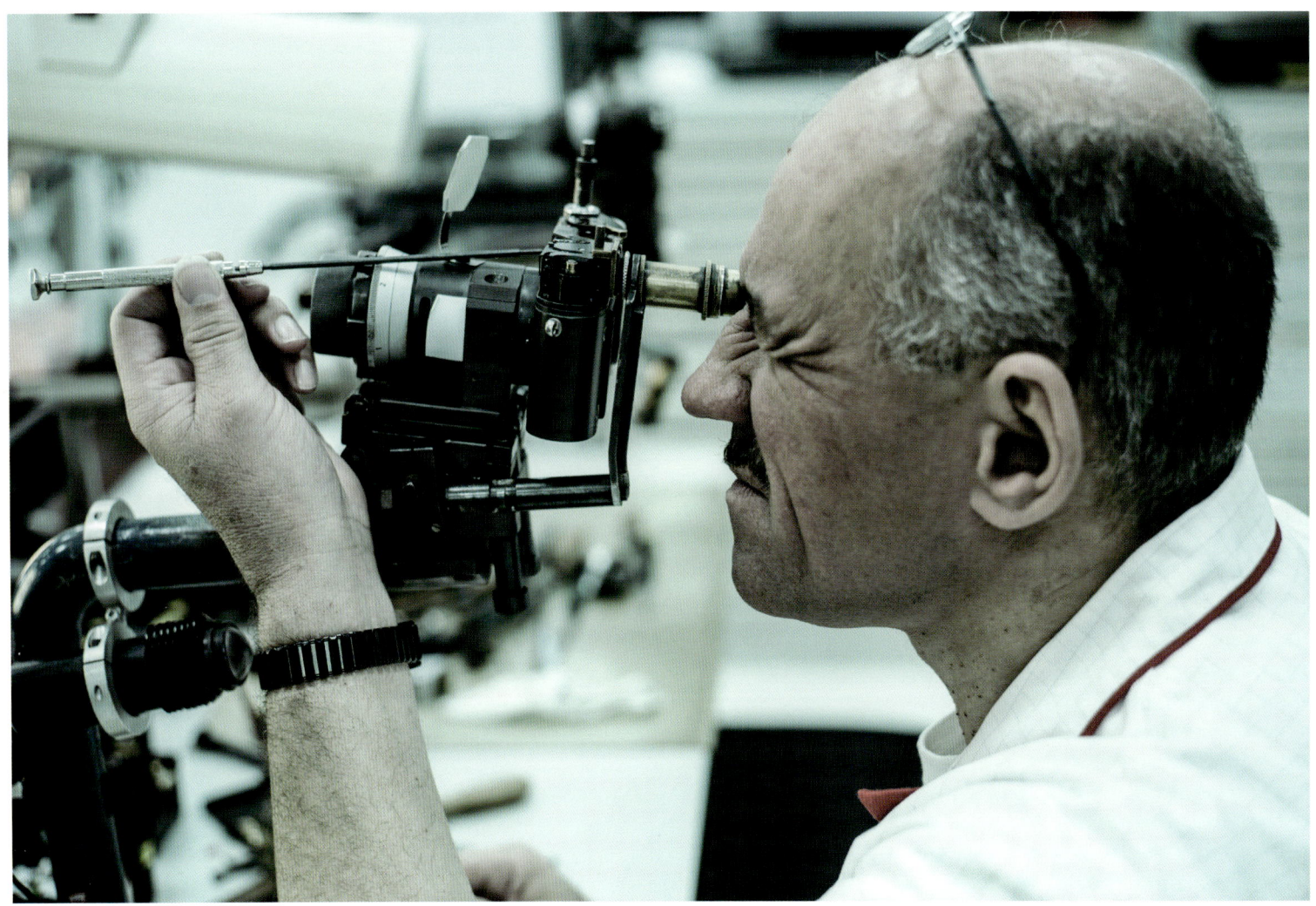

Siegbert Merz is an analog camera expert. This image shows him adjusting the rangefinder mechanism using a screw that is usually hidden behind the famous red dot.

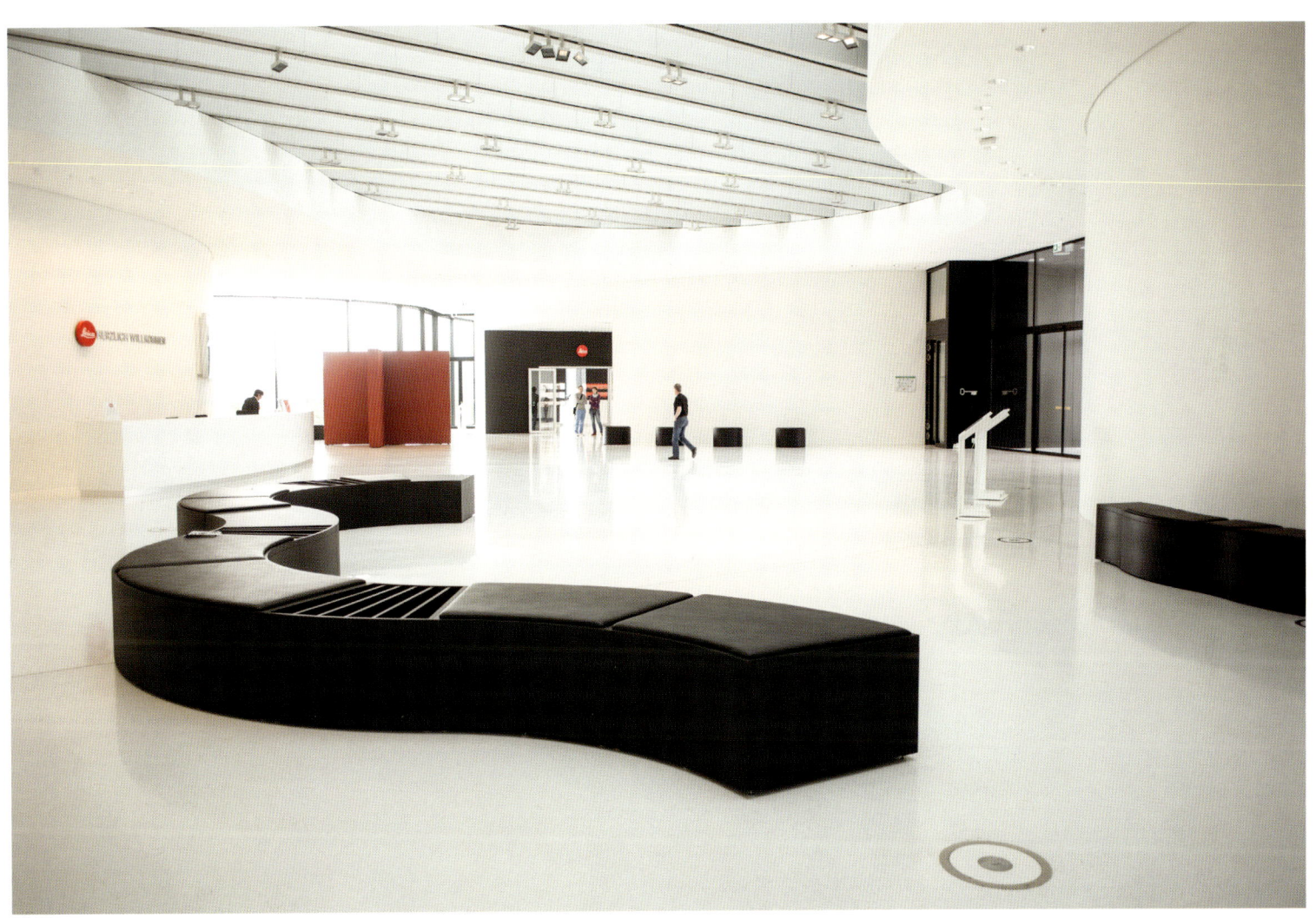

The modern reception hall is the starting point for all visitors to the Leica building.
Café Leitz is located just across from the main foyer.

3.   The Leica Rangefinder
Uses and Limitations

I know you really want to get out and start taking photos, but there is still one technical aspect of the Leica M we need to look at. The rangefinder is the single most important element of the Leica-based composition process, so it is essential to take a close look at how it works.

Opinions on the Leica rangefinder are divided: Some see it as a clunky anachronism while others see it as the ultimate photographic tool. Whatever you think, the rangefinder is a masterpiece of mechanical engineering. So how does a rangefinder work? Unlike with a single lens reflex (SLR) camera with which the photographer views the subject directly through the lens by way of a mirror and a pentaprism, a Leica photographer views a scene through the viewfinder window built into the upper-left corner of the camera body.

In high-quality SLRs, the viewfinder covers up to 100 percent of the frame. In contrast, the rectangle displayed in the Leica viewfinder gives only a general indication of the framing that will appear in the final image. In an SLR, the effect of swapping lenses is immediately and completely visible in the viewfinder, whereas in a Leica, it is only the size of the Bright-line frame that changes while the overall viewfinder image remains the same.

Using an SLR, you can focus anywhere within the frame, whereas with a Leica, you can only use the dedicated rectangle in the center of the Bright-line frame. Don't worry, I'm not going to explain precisely how the rangefinder works—that would be confusing and wouldn't help you take better pictures or increase your enjoyment of photography. There is only one thing you really have to remember: If the window located beneath the shutter speed dial is covered, you won't be able to measure distances or focus successfully.

How Does the Leica Viewfinder Affect Our Photography?

As I already mentioned, macro and telephoto photography are not a Leica's strong points. In the case of telephoto lenses, the longer the lens, the smaller the rangefinder window in the viewfinder, which makes precise focusing increasingly difficult.

The camera's design means that the rangefinder window has to be placed several centimeters away from the viewfinder, so at subject distances of less than 70cm (about 28 inches), the parallax effect is too great for accurate framing. To see the parallax effect for yourself, hold up your index finger, move it about two feet away from your face and then look at it with your right eye (with your left eye closed) and then with your left eye (with your right eye closed). You will see that your finger appears to jump sideways when you switch eyes. In this case, the cause of the effect is the distance between your eyes rather than the distance between the viewfinder and rangefinder windows.

Forget macro and telephoto shots. Few of us need a universal do-it-all camera, just as we don't use a screwdriver to drive in a nail or a hammer to affix a screw. Instead, let's talk about the advantages of the rangefinder system.

The rangefinder makes smaller cameras possible and correspondingly compact lenses with improved optical correction. Because a rangefinder camera has no mirror, lenses can be designed to sit closer to the sensor or film; and because there are no mirror movements involved, the camera is quieter. These are all good reasons to use this type of camera for documentary photography of human subjects. Leica cameras remain the tool of choice for many members of the Magnum agency, and other famous photographers. Henri Cartier-Bresson used a Leica to perfect his highly personal style of candid street photography.

Using Your Leica

Now that we've got all that out of the way, let's take some photos. Pick up your camera, rest your right index finger on the shutter release button, support the camera body with your left hand and grasp the focusing ring with your left thumb and index finger. If you raise the camera to your right eye, you can rest your left arm against your ribs. Using your right eye to focus prevents your nose from interfering with the camera and helps to avoid grease marks on the monitor. You can now frame your subject in the Bright-line frame in the viewfinder.

If you want to know why I attach such importance to posture, just take a look at a bunch of tourists at any popular site. They usually hold their camera at any old angle in one hand and a bottle of water in the other. The chance of the photos they shoot coming out well is more a matter of luck than intent. My aim is to spot as many sources of shooting errors as possible and eliminate them.

The more firmly and securely you hold your camera, the less risk there is of your images coming out blurred and the better you can concentrate on framing your subject. Place your subject within the Bright-line frame and take a step forward or to the side. Move your body to frame the subject and, when you are satisfied with your composition, use the split-image rectangle to focus. Your subject doesn't have to be in the center of the frame just because the focusing rectangle is positioned there.

A Small Tip

If you are working at maximum aperture (often a good idea when you are shooting with a Leica M), remember not to rotate or tip the camera once you have set focus. Only move the camera left, right, up, or down in the plane you have focused on; otherwise, you run the risk of losing the focus and spoiling your image.

Optimal Focus for a Portrait

If you are shooting portraits, typically the best thing to focus on is the eye or the side of the subject's face that is closest to the camera, although the best spot can vary depending on the type of lens you are using and the camera-to-subject distance. You don't have to take as much care focusing if you use a wide-angle lens at a relatively large distance, but things get trickier if you are using a bright standard or telephoto lens at maximum aperture to shoot a portrait of someone close by. A portrait with in-focus nostrils or ears but blurred eyes is no use to anyone.

Focusing on Close-Ups

If you are shooting a close-up portrait using a standard lens set to its maximum aperture, you will be working close to the minimum focus distance, so setting focus using the focus ring on the lens doesn't always work. Because you and your subject are never perfectly still, adjusting the focus ring increases the potential for focus errors. I prefer to frame my subject, set a fixed distance, and then fine-tune focus by moving my body carefully back and forth. I release the shutter every time the split image in the viewfinder indicates correct focus. Try it for yourself—the number of sharp images you capture is sure to increase.

Use your left eye to observe what's going on around you while you shoot. This way, you have a head start on objects moving from left to right and you will be able to release the shutter at precisely the right moment. It takes a little practice to keep one eye on the viewfinder while you use the other to scan for subjects, but the Leica system makes this approach easy. Fast-moving subjects, too, are simpler to capture, although doing so by adjusting the focus ring while panning often produces blurred results. Pre-focusing on a stationary object such as the surface of a road or a bush located at an appropriate distance is much more reliable. Because you can keep an eye on your surroundings, the Leica viewfinder system makes capturing great photos easier.

Another Valuable Tip

Once you have finished shooting a particular subject, it is a good idea to set focus to infinity. This way, you only ever move the focus ring to the right and you won't usually have to move it as far as you would if you start from the other end of the scale.

You are correct if you think that you can't work as precisely with a Leica as you can with a high-end SLR, but there is no other camera in the world that enables you to work as quickly and intuitively. But what makes a great image great? Is it one that is level, well framed, and in focus? Doesn't that sound like a recipe for a humdrum, everyday snapshot? A great photo isn't necessarily technically perfect, even if plenty of textbooks would have us believe otherwise. A great photo can break any number of rules. An exciting image can have a sloping horizon, and an interesting image doesn't have to make sense at a glance. We will be taking a closer look at the aspects of good photography later on.

Photo Exercise #3

What you need: Your Leica, a 35mm or 50mm lens, film or a memory card. Find a street scene and use the technique described above to capture images of moving cars or bicycles in sharp focus in the center of the frame. Try out various apertures, shutter speeds, and distance settings.

German Angst

As you know, I earn my living taking photographs. I have a lot of fun doing my job, but it is a challenge to find the right content; it makes great demands on my time, too. Nevertheless, I still like to tackle topics that don't necessarily promise a financial return but that give me the freedom to work without the pressure of deadlines or a client's demands.

Following the Fukushima disaster in 2011, I began work on a project I call "German Angst." This phrase is often used in English-speaking countries to characterize behavior seen by outsiders as "typically German," including characteristics such as hesitancy, fastidiousness, and caution. For example, the events in Fukushima appeared to produce a much greater feeling of anxiety in the Germans than it did in the Japanese, and I began to ask myself why.

My research came up with very little literature on the subject, although for the past 25 years a large insurance company has conducted an annual survey into the greatest German fears, and a handful of authors have expressed their thoughts on the subject in books and magazine articles. This lack of information didn't provide me with a solid foundation to work

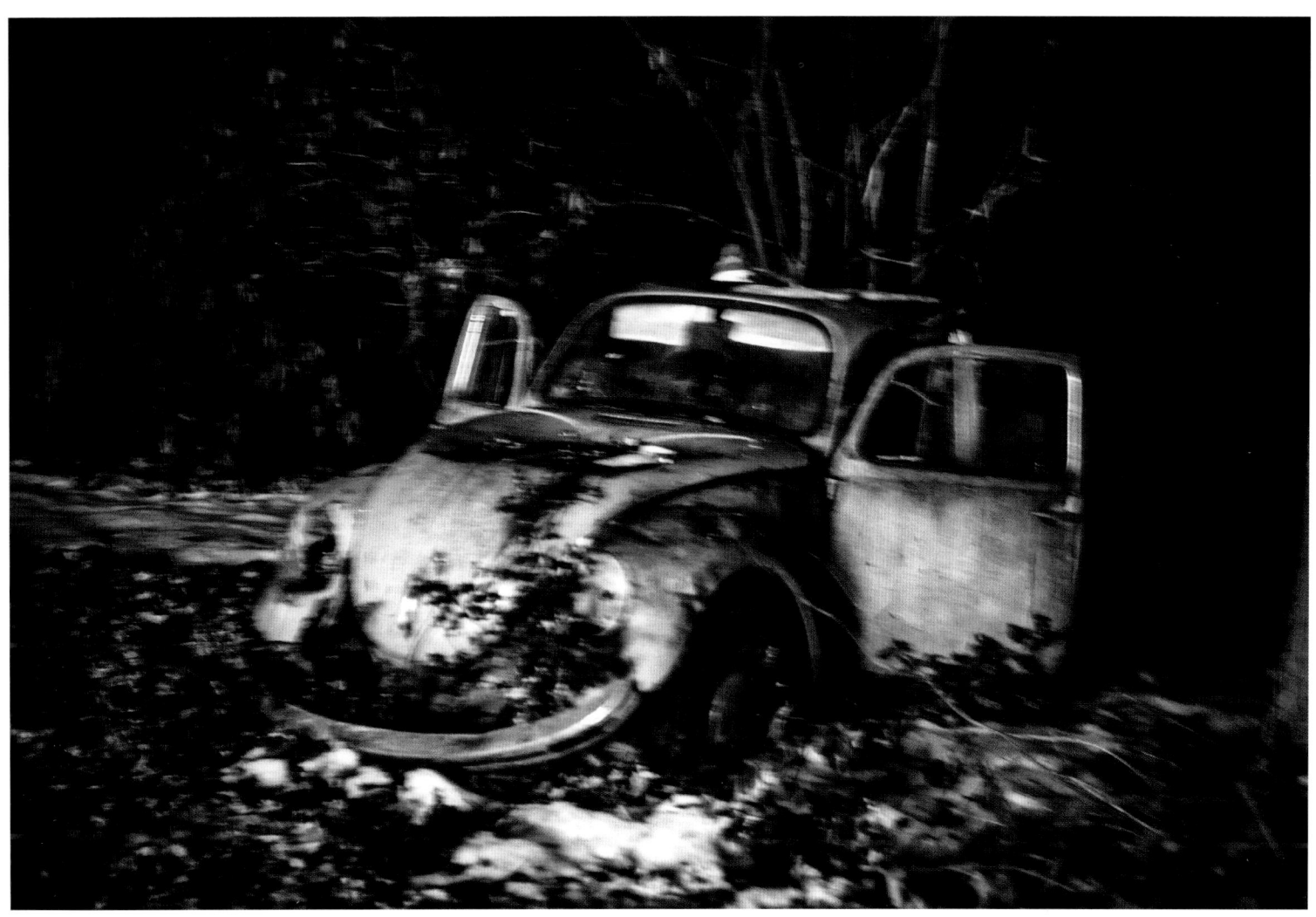

In the glow of an Easter bonfire in Hamburg
M9, f/2, 1/8 s, ISO 640, 35mm

on, but gave me the inspiration I needed to find out for myself. I decided to delve photographically into the "Germanness" of the Germans in a personal and subjective way.

The aim of this project is not to explain anything, but rather to get my viewers thinking. The result is a sequence of images that amuse, confuse, and often raise unanswered questions. Everyone should form their own opinions about what these images mean.

They were created using my M9 and Typ 240 bodies and lenses with focal lengths between 21mm and 75mm.

In the end, I even managed to make some money with the project, thanks to financial support from the Kulturwerk trust run by the VG Bild-Kunst artists' association.

Don't pay too much attention to the captions—just have fun letting your imagination run free.

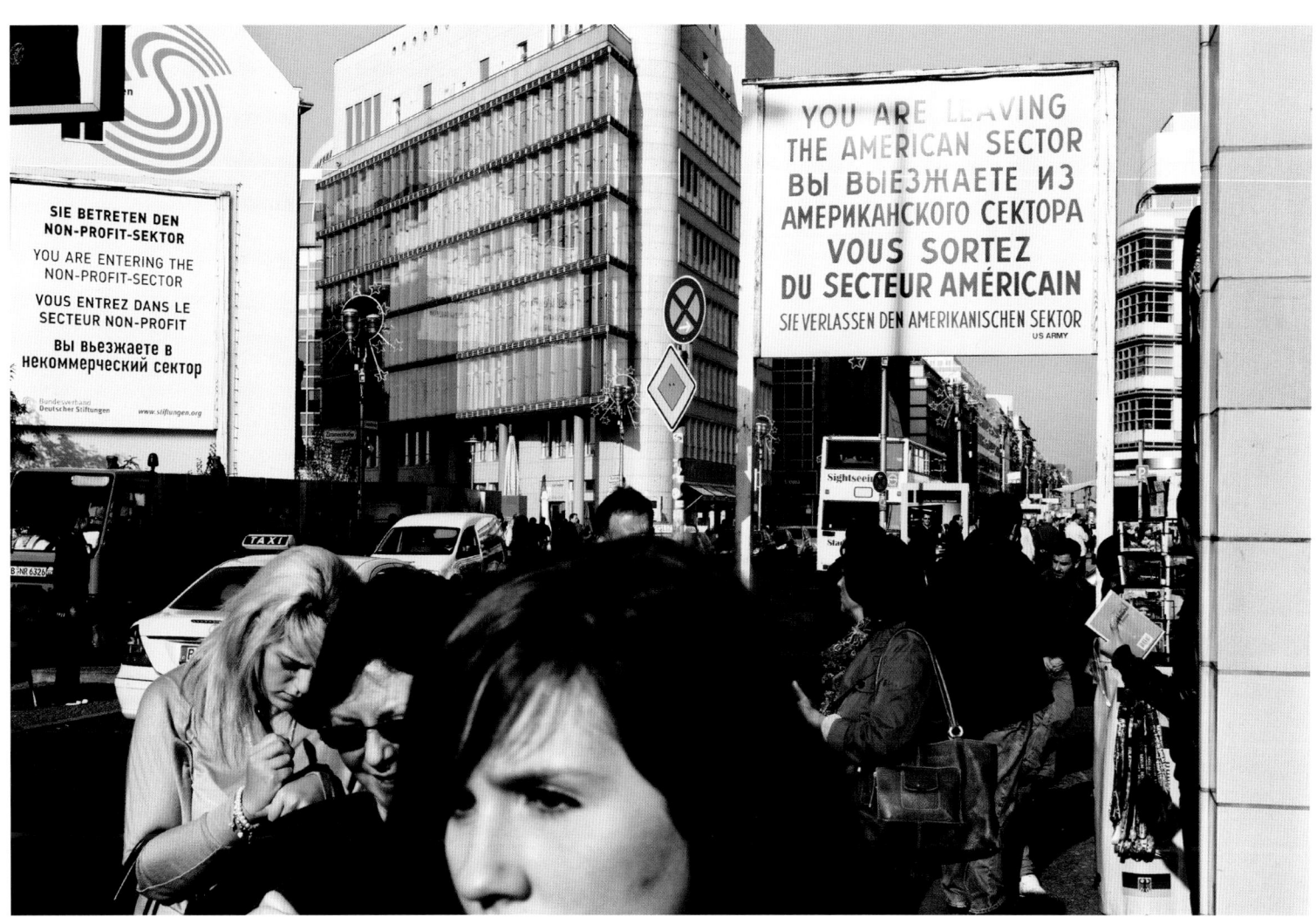

Checkpoint Charlie, Berlin
M9, f/16, 1/500 s, ISO 320, 35mm

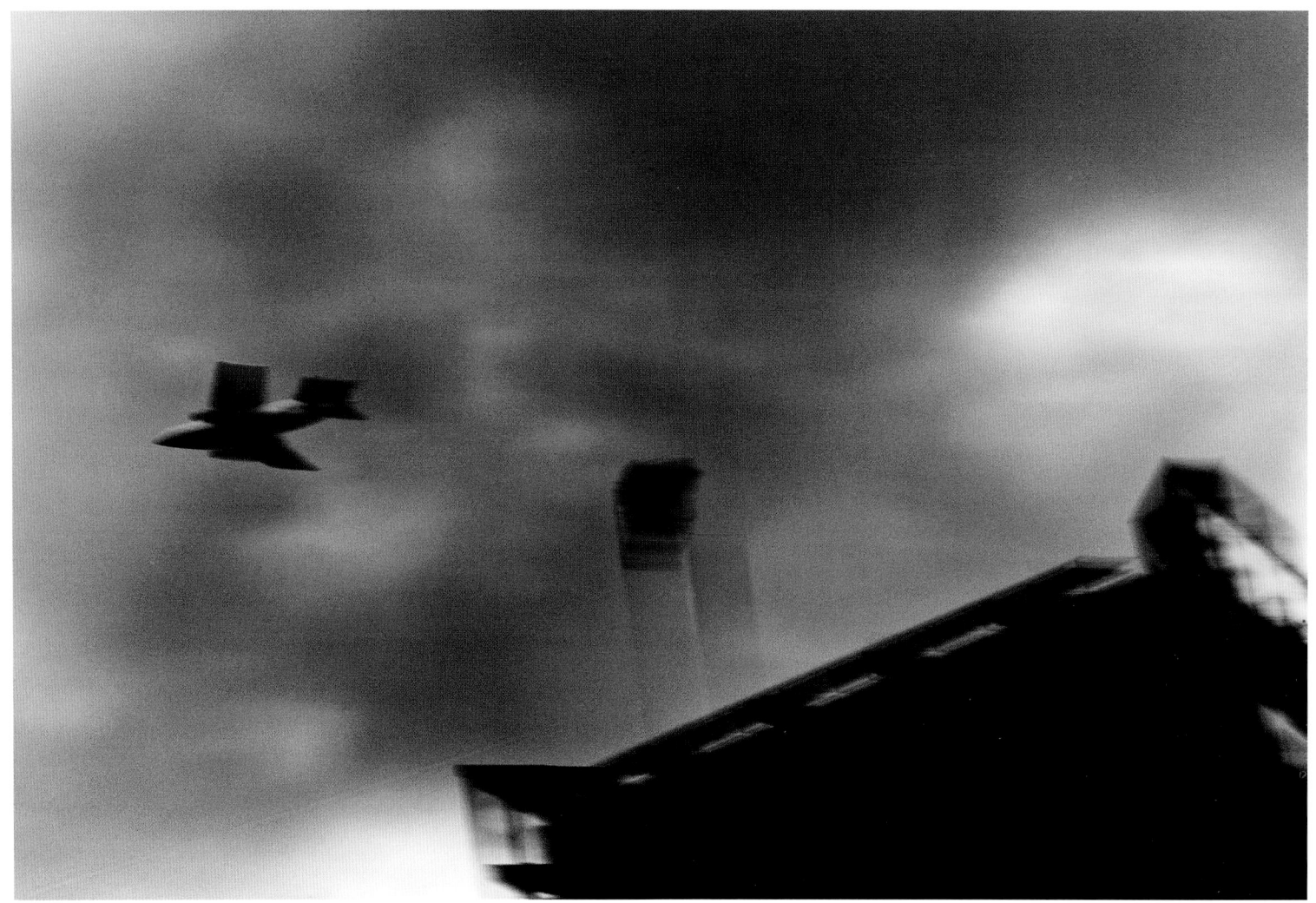

The port of Hamburg
M8, f/4, 1/30 s, ISO 160, 75mm

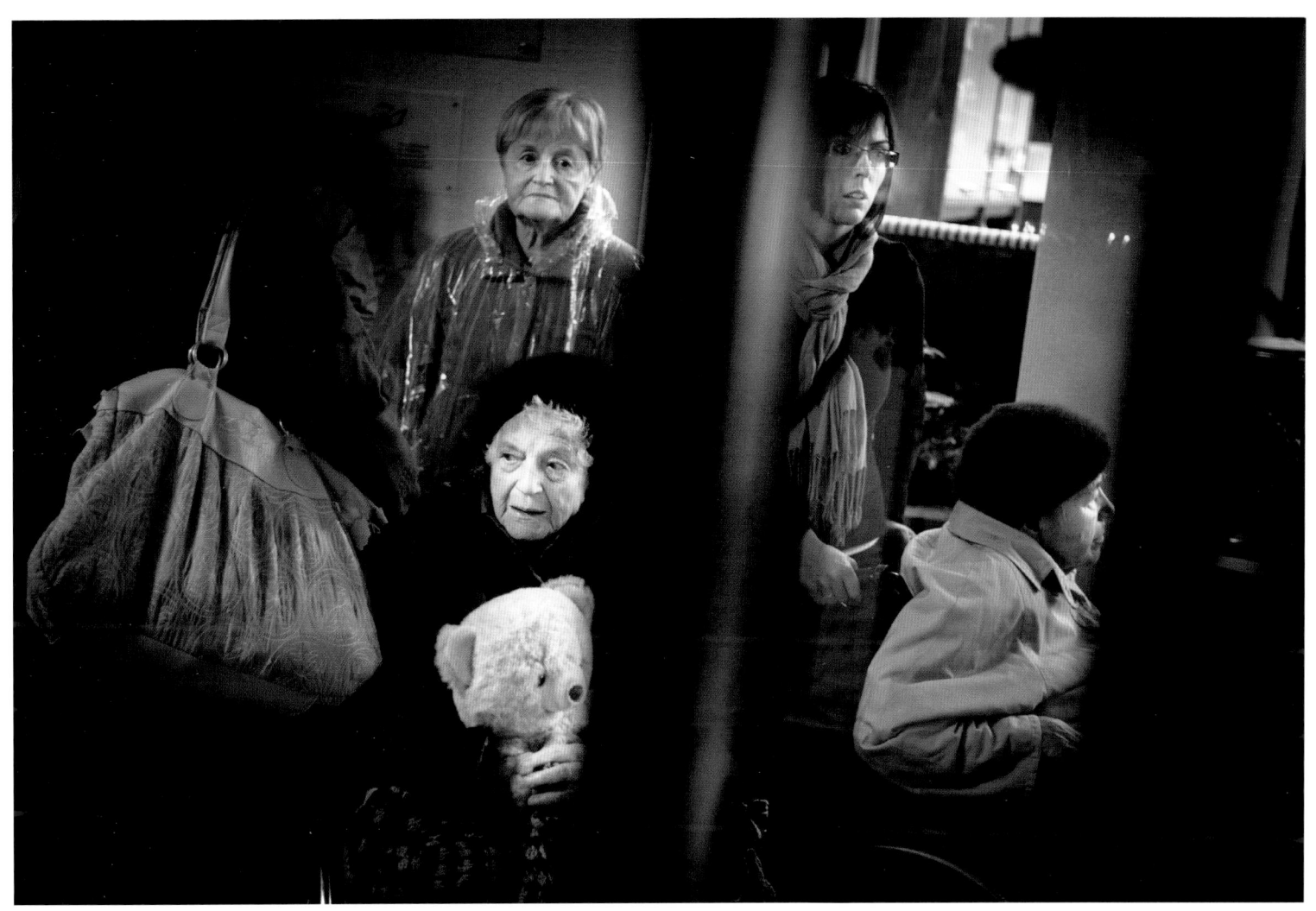

Evacuating a retirement home in Koblenz because of an unexploded wartime bomb
M9, f/2, 1/60 s, ISO 640, 50mm

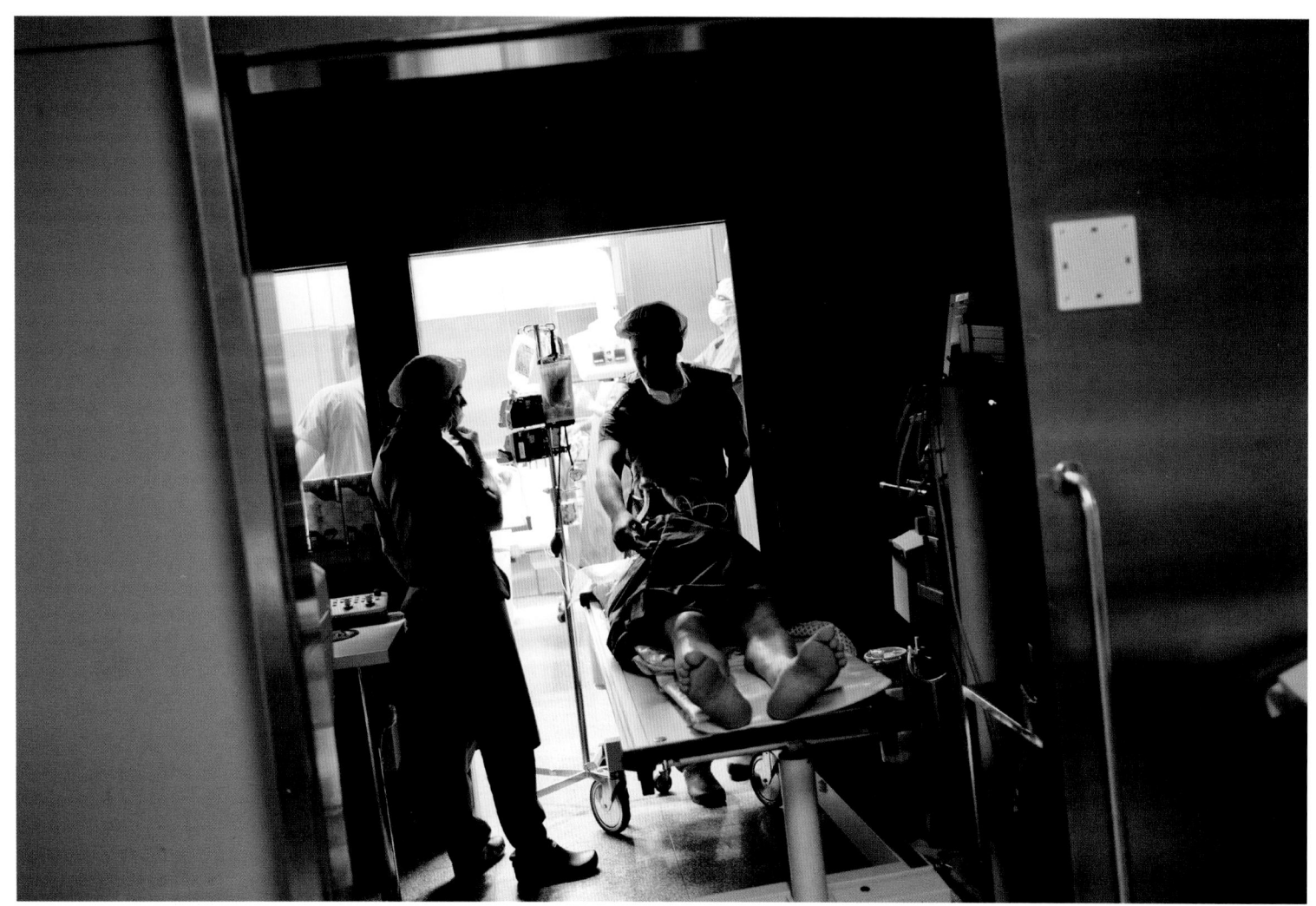

Surgery in Kiel
M9, f/2, 1/60 s, ISO 800, 35 mm

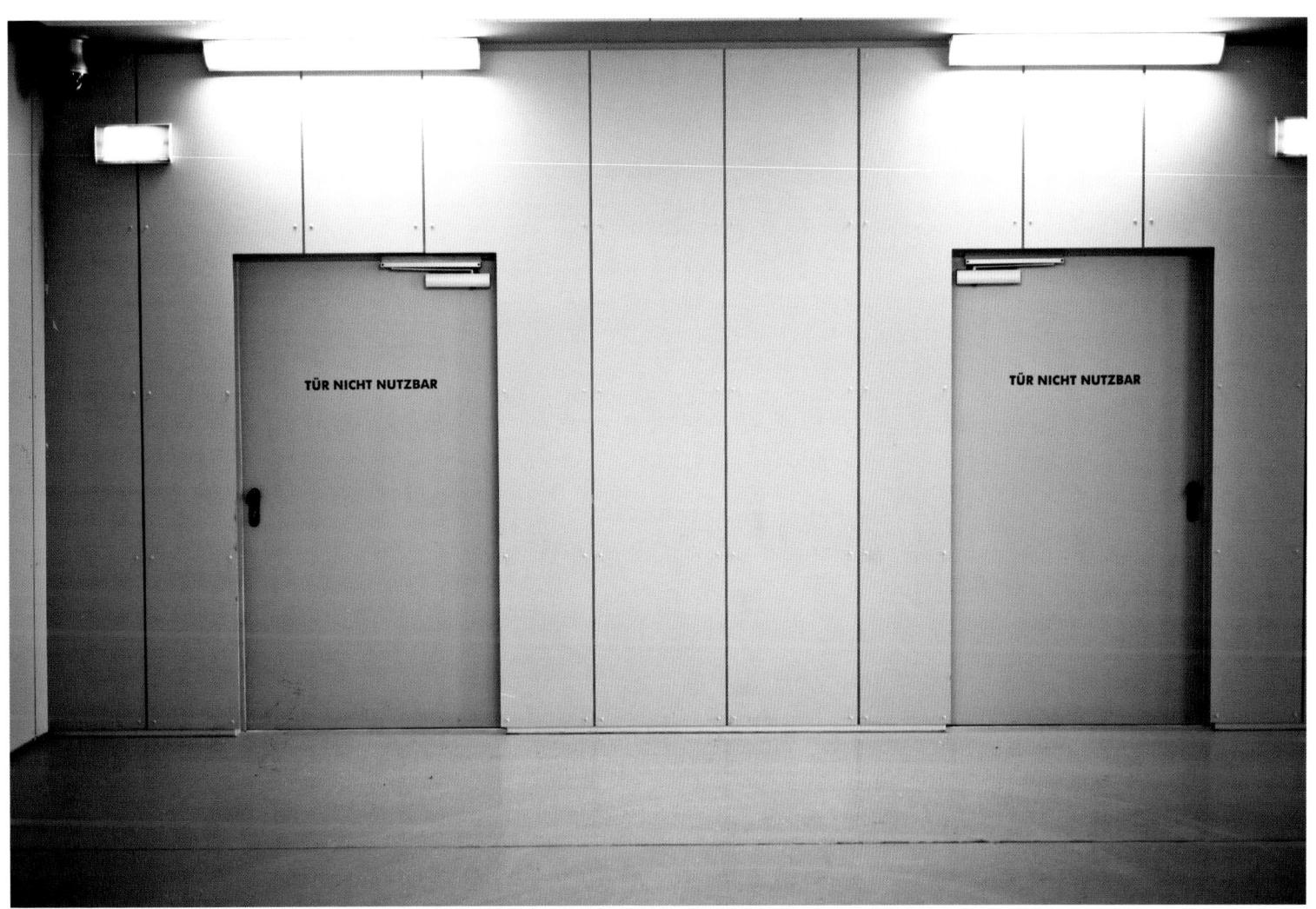

A shopping mall in Oberhausen
M9, f/2.8, 1/60 s, ISO 400, 50mm

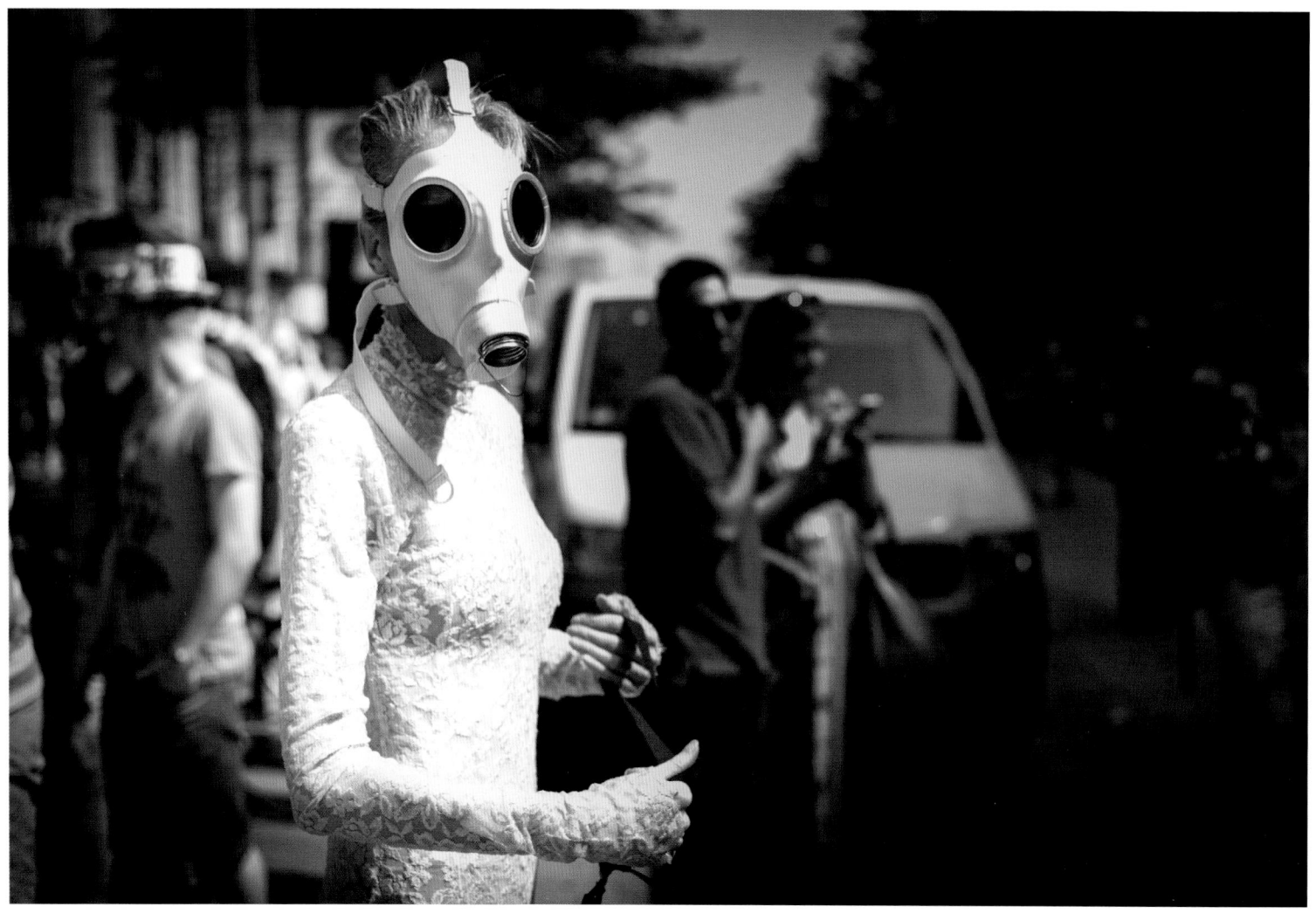

Hamburg – Christopher Street Day
M240, f/2, 1/500 s, ISO 200, 50mm, ND Filter

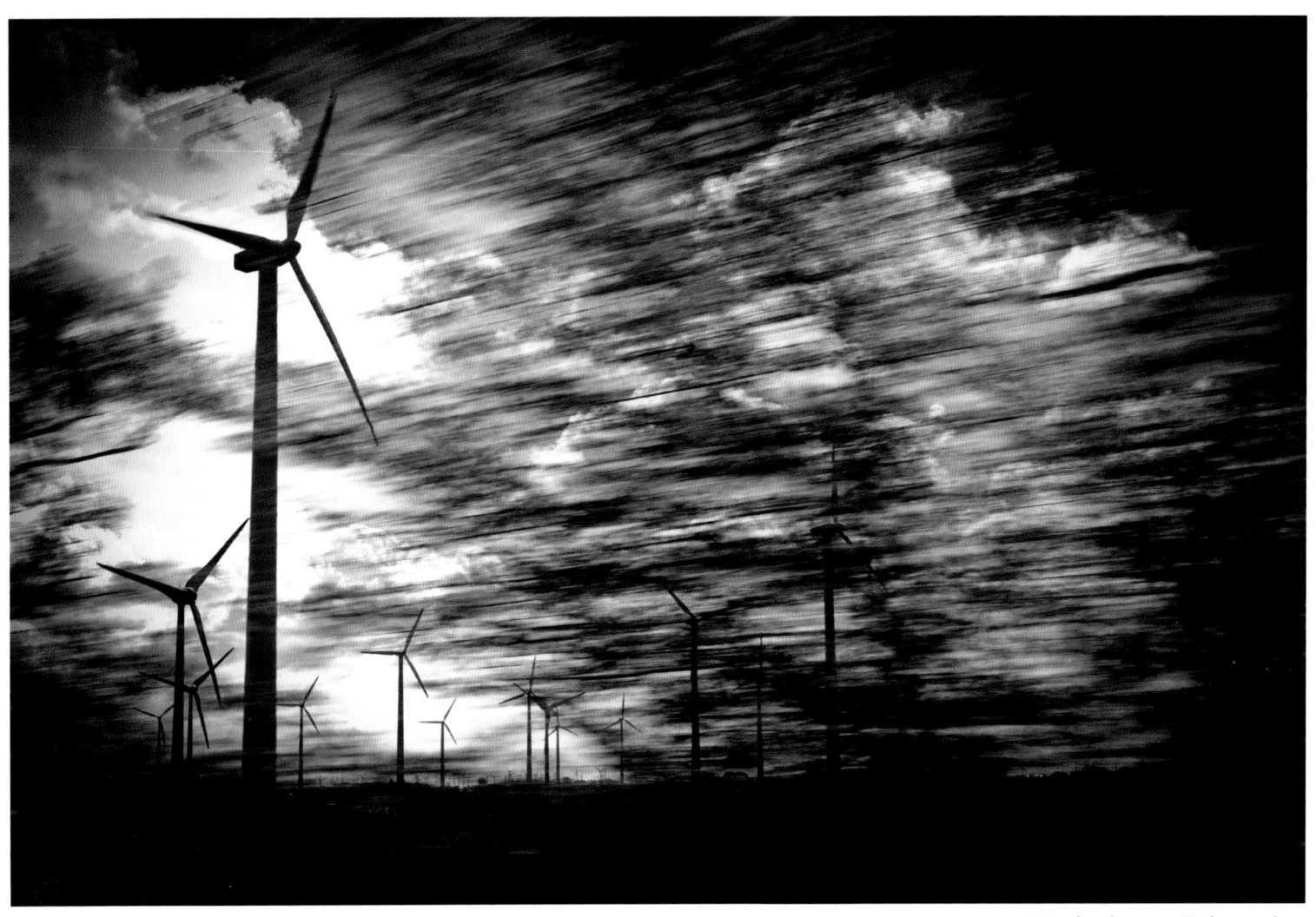

Wind turbines in Dithmarschen
M9, f/22, 1/60 s, ISO 160, 50mm, shot from my car

4.   The Crucial Shot

From a Single Image to a Complete Story

Are you ready to take some photos? You are now familiar with the technical aspects of your camera and lenses, but that is only half of the story. Technology alone doesn't guarantee successful images.

Have you ever heard of a famous author who attributes the success of a book to a particular type of pen? Or a musician who cites a specific brand of instrument as the fount of his virtuosity? I am sure you would agree this is rarely the case. Of course, many artists have emotional ties to the tools they use and their tools can vary in their suitability for the job.

The same is true for photographers. A particular type of camera can be perfect for the assignment at hand and may provoke an emotional reaction in the photographer. People often see a kind of cause-and-effect relationship between photographers and the cameras they use, and interpret this as the basis for the quality of the resulting photos. Many camera buyers still seem to think that they will automatically produce great pictures if they use a renowned camera from an established manufacturer—but believe me, this is not the case!

So you have acquired a Leica M, perhaps in spite of or perhaps because of its limitations. You have already reached an emotional decision by making your purchase and, in doing so, you have become a member of the Leica community—a distinction that means you will regularly find yourself having to justify why you use the apparent anachronism you are carrying. But we don't mind all that; we simply want to get out and shoot some photos.

So what do you want to photograph? Are you going to head out and wait for your images to happen? What kinds of images are you waiting for?

You know how it is when you are toying with the idea of buying a new car: you suddenly see the model you are thinking about everywhere you go. Or you are thinking about where to go on your next vacation and every conversation you have or magazine article you read is about the same destination. Is this a coincidence? Of course not!

The fact that you are thinking about a specific topic increases your awareness of it and you react to stimuli that were previously uninteresting, even though the actual number of stimuli hasn't changed.

From a photographer's point of view, once you have decided on a theme, simply waiting for photos to happen makes no sense. You may get lucky and stumble across an interesting subject or two, but you won't be in control of the situation.

A while ago, I bought Peter Turnley's book *French Kiss*, which is basically a declaration of love for the city of Paris and is full of images of kissing couples. My first thought on leafing through the book was that my home city is nothing like the French capital, but I quickly found that Hamburg, too, is full of kissing couples—I just hadn't noticed before.

What Does All this Have to Do with Our Special Kind of Photography?

And why am I so keen to get you thinking this way? Capturing individual images that please you is a great start but is probably not going to satisfy you in the long run. You have acquired a camera that begs like no other to be used for reportage: a discipline seen by many as the ultimate photographic challenge.

But before we go too far, let's take a look at what the term reportage really means. What is the difference between a single image and a multi-image story, and does arranging images in a sequence automatically make them reportage?

Reportage-style photography is always based on a sequence of images and has an overriding theme that gives the sequence a degree of innate coherence. Put simply: Reportage tells a story in pictures.

How to Tell a Story

There are as many ways to tell a story as there are stories. You can shoot in black-and-white or color. You can stick to a single lens or you can vary your angle of view. You can select a particular perspective or vary your viewpoint from shot to shot. You can work exclusively with available light or shoot using flash and other artificial light sources. There are endless technical options when it comes to building up a photographic story.

There are just as many options when it comes to content: You can tell a story by following an event as it unfolds, or by taking a serial approach that includes a single theme or object in each shot of a sequence. For example, when Pope John Paul I died, the world's top-flight photojournalists descended on Rome to photograph the events taking place in and around the Vatican. The events themselves were the theme. Magnum photographer Paolo Pellegrin took a different approach, putting more emphasis on the grieving faithful. The result was an incredibly moving photo story, which he called "Vigil at St. Peter's Square," and which is a great example of the serial approach to reportage photography.

Your job is to decide which technical and stylistic devices you want to use to tell your own story. Do you already know which story you want to tell?

I was fortunate to find my way slowly into the world of reportage photography through my work as a photojournalist. When I was starting out, I was sent off to cover low-profile events where there wasn't much that could go wrong. The important thing was that I brought back a well-exposed, in-focus image. However, I soon discovered that the more images I captured, the more ended up in print. This encouraged me to start covering events from a variety of angles using different perspectives and a range of lenses. During this period, I learned much from my editorial colleagues who had begun their careers taking photos, as they pointed out what a story lacked and what I could do better. This all meant that I was given specific dates and clear guidance regarding the themes I was sent to photograph.

The following sections are intended to help you find your own stories without the editorial support that I enjoyed, regardless of whether you are working professionally or simply brushing up your photo skills as a hobbyist.

Developing Your Own Story

I am assuming that nobody is giving you assignments, there are no financial goals involved, and you can photograph whatever you like. This is a relaxed place to start from, but are you really relaxed? Or have you discovered that it's not as simple as you thought to come up with a story?

It's actually quite hard to find and photograph good stories among the everyday events that surround us. You could, of course, put off starting until your next vacation, but don't you want to get started right away?

Where can you look for a story when life around you is so normal? A good place to start is a family event such as a birthday party, a wedding, or a christening that you can photograph from start to finish. You can document an event like this as an outsider looking in, or you can shoot from the point of view of the main protagonist. The advantage of shooting at a family event is that it will probably only take a day or two; the downside is that you are likely to be so busy shooting that you will miss the party. Another good place to start is in your own neighborhood. Try starting a long-term documentary project about life around a busy square or park. Or how about recording life at a shopping center in your area? You can also use the unspoken trust between yourself and your partner, children, or other members of your family as the basis for a photo sequence. All that really matters is the basic idea and your will to succeed. You needn't be afraid to rework ideas that other photographers have already used. It is extremely unlikely that you will ever find a subject that hasn't been photographed many times before.

What makes your story unique is you. Your knowledge, your experience, your hopes, and your fears are yours alone, and they form the basis of your highly personal view of the world. This is the foundation on which to build your work.

Just as kissing couples form the binding element in *French Kiss*, a repeated element such as people using mobile phones, or inanimate objects such as car parks (an idea realized by Magnum photographer Martin Parr) can be the sparks that inspire a story. Elliott Erwitt (another Magnum photographer) shot a series of photos of people visiting museums, although his most famous photos have dogs as their common subject. I often go to polo matches and photograph life off the field; documenting my hometown of Hamburg is another of my long-term projects. The latter is not a traditional city documentary but rather a highly personal view of the place where I live. I don't try to show the city from its best side and I certainly don't aim to produce images that will please everyone. My main motivation is to express my own emotions in pictures. For the last 12 years, I have also been documenting my daughter's development. I make an annual photo calendar for friends and relatives, and I have even considered giving her a book of her own life for her 18th birthday.

I am always working on several projects at a time, some of which are easier to plan than others. Though they may differ in their approaches and the stories they convey, I enjoy all of my projects. They all have a personal element and nobody has to motivate me to carry on with my work.

You can only create truly great images if the story you are telling affects you personally. I will talk some more about how to find the personal angle in the next chapter.

Photo Exercise #4

Take a look at several photo books and magazines. Try to discover why some stories appeal to you and others don't. Look closely and analyze the sequences of images involved. Consider the viewpoints the photographers have chosen and try to discern the type of lens they used to capture each image.

The St. Pauli Piers

This reportage gives you a taste of life at the famous landing piers in the St. Pauli quarter of Hamburg. In contrast to the long-term projects introduced in other chapters, I shot this sequence in one day especially for this book. The fact that Leica had loaned me an M Monochrom to test was all the encouragement I needed to get out and shoot a new story. This sequence is also designed to demonstrate that you don't need to travel far or visit spectacular events to produce exciting images. The St. Pauli Piers are a public space and it was easy to find out a little about their history. While you shoot, keep the journalist's five "W" questions in mind: Who? What? When? Where? Why? You won't always be able to answer them all photographically, but they provide a good set of guidelines. My gear consisted of the M Monochrom, my M9 as a backup, and my 35mm and 50mm lenses. My bag was so

light I was able to leave the car at home and travel by subway to my chosen location. Looking for a parking space can be a chore and can seriously spoil your mood before you even begin to shoot. The St. Pauli Piers are also accessible by public ferry, so I was able to shoot from the water, too. This partially answered the "where" question, although the weather was poor and I wasn't able to capture the overview I was hoping to snap from the boat.

Back on land, I did some reconnaissance at the water's edge with my camera at the ready. I noticed a man selling tickets for harbor tours ("who"), some palm trees a café owner had set up on one of the pontoons, as well as seagulls, ducks, food stalls, countless boats, and even more tourists ("what"). At this point I concentrated on trying to register new impressions rather than falling back into old habits. The weather

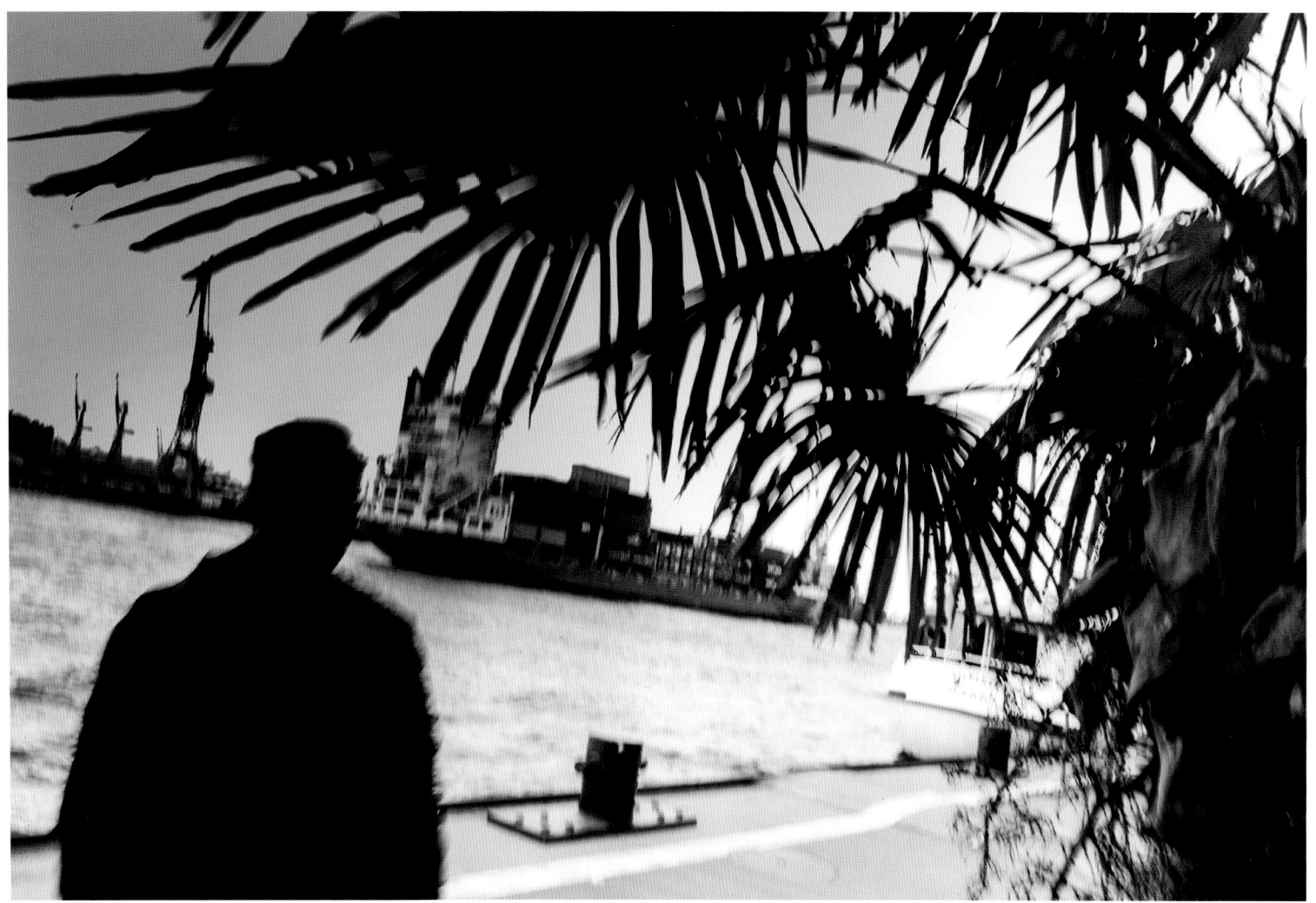

Palm trees in Hamburg are an unusual sight. The surreal effect is underscored by the deliberate blur, while the sloped composition increases the tension.

wasn't particularly good, but do we really need blue sky and sunshine to take photos? Great photos depend on what you make of the situation you find yourself in. Rain, mist, and diffuse light all have their own special charm if you are prepared to open your mind and immerse yourself in your surroundings.

The next step involved forming a plan from all the things I had observed. The palm trees had a bizarre effect that I really wanted to capture. The piers themselves were often reflected in the windows of the tourist boats, making an interesting subject with people involved, too. I waited for one of the boats to land and hoped to catch a moment with plenty going on. On this particular day I was lucky.

Fish sandwiches are an integral part of the St. Pauli Piers experience and were top of my list of must-have subjects. I really wanted to get some shots of a heavily tattooed woman selling the sandwiches, but I couldn't gain her attention, which was a shame. She remained dismissive, even when I bought a sandwich, and then when she put on a jacket, the moment was lost. I took some shots of the ducks, although I wasn't particularly happy with the results.

The man selling tickets for harbor tours made up for the disappointment and he didn't hesitate to give me permission to photograph him. We chatted for a while and he told me some of his life story while I snapped away. Although I observed him quite closely, he didn't want to tell me his real name: "Everyone here calls me Captain Birdseye!" A few days later, I went back and gave him a print of one my shots.

Now all I needed was the "where." I moved away from the water and took some shots of the old warehouse building with its distinctive clock tower and famous water level indicator. The results won't win any prizes, but at least the shot includes the "when," too. The only thing missing was the "why," and that was easily answered by the hours I spent getting to know the piers and their people. Shooting this story was a lot of fun and sifting through the images that evening made me really happy.

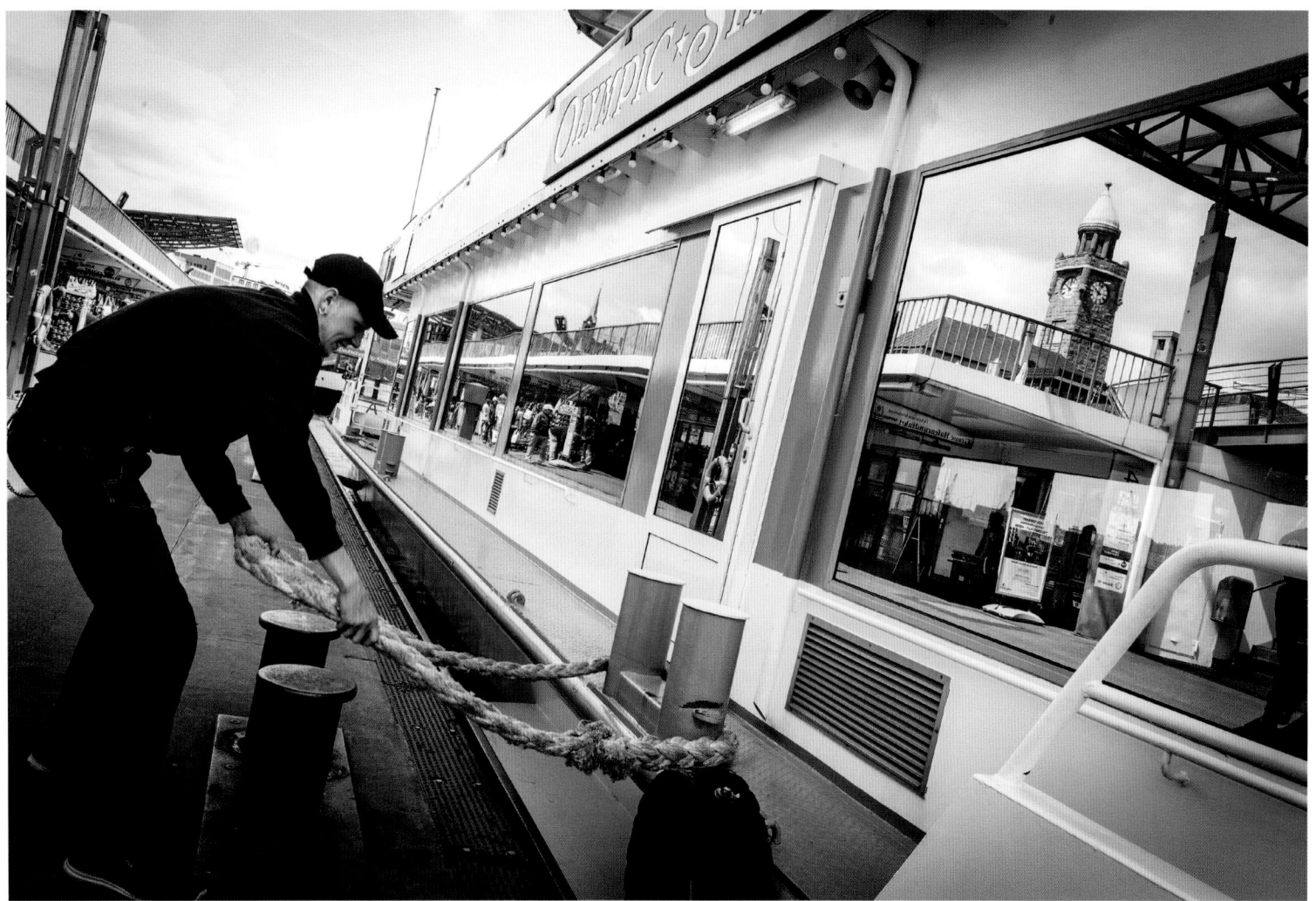

The reflections of the piers in the windows of the boat introduce a third dimension into the frame. The dominant lines of the composition all lead to the man hauling the rope, giving this image a clean but interesting look.

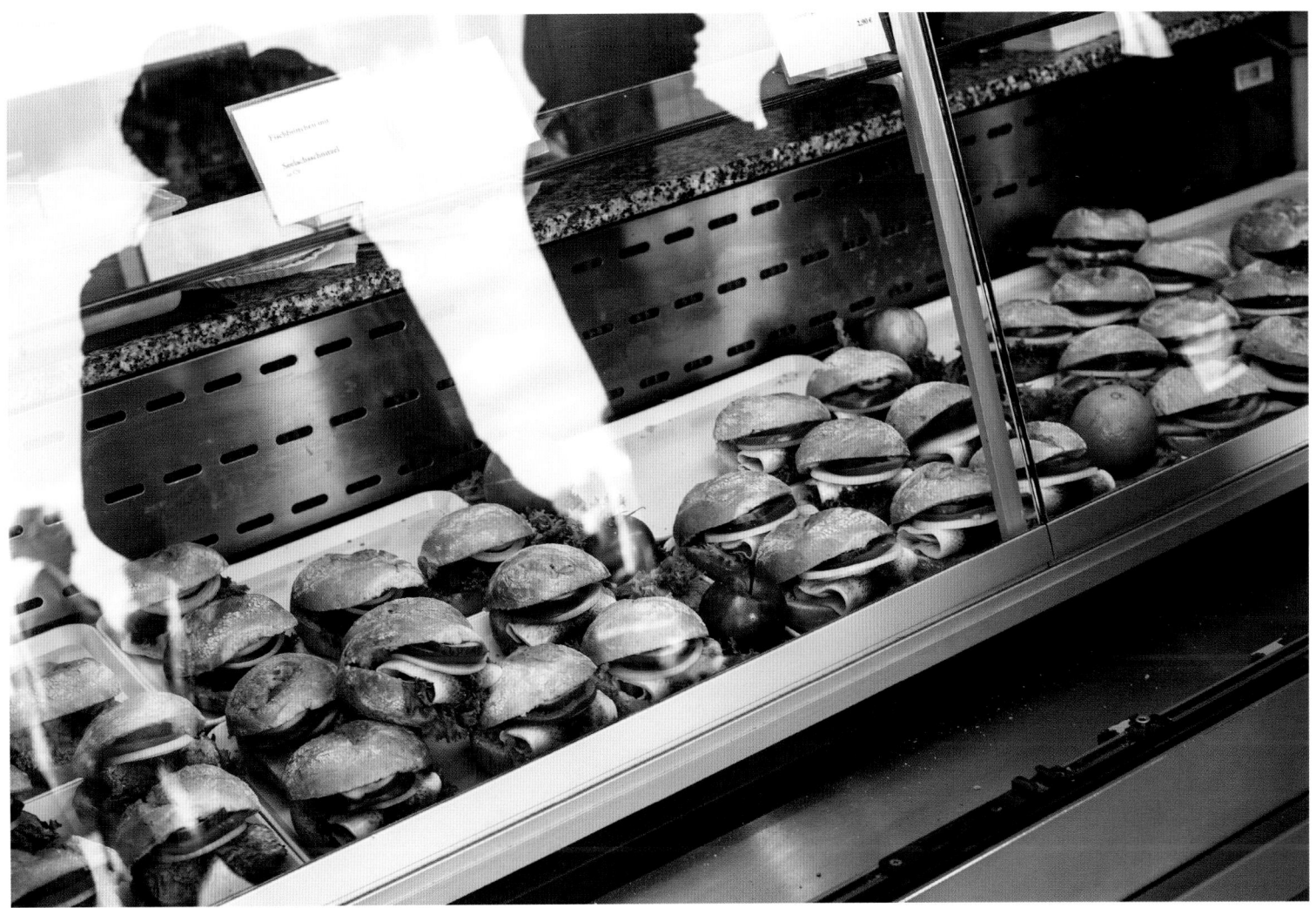

The reflections of people waiting to buy fish sandwiches add visual and contextual depth

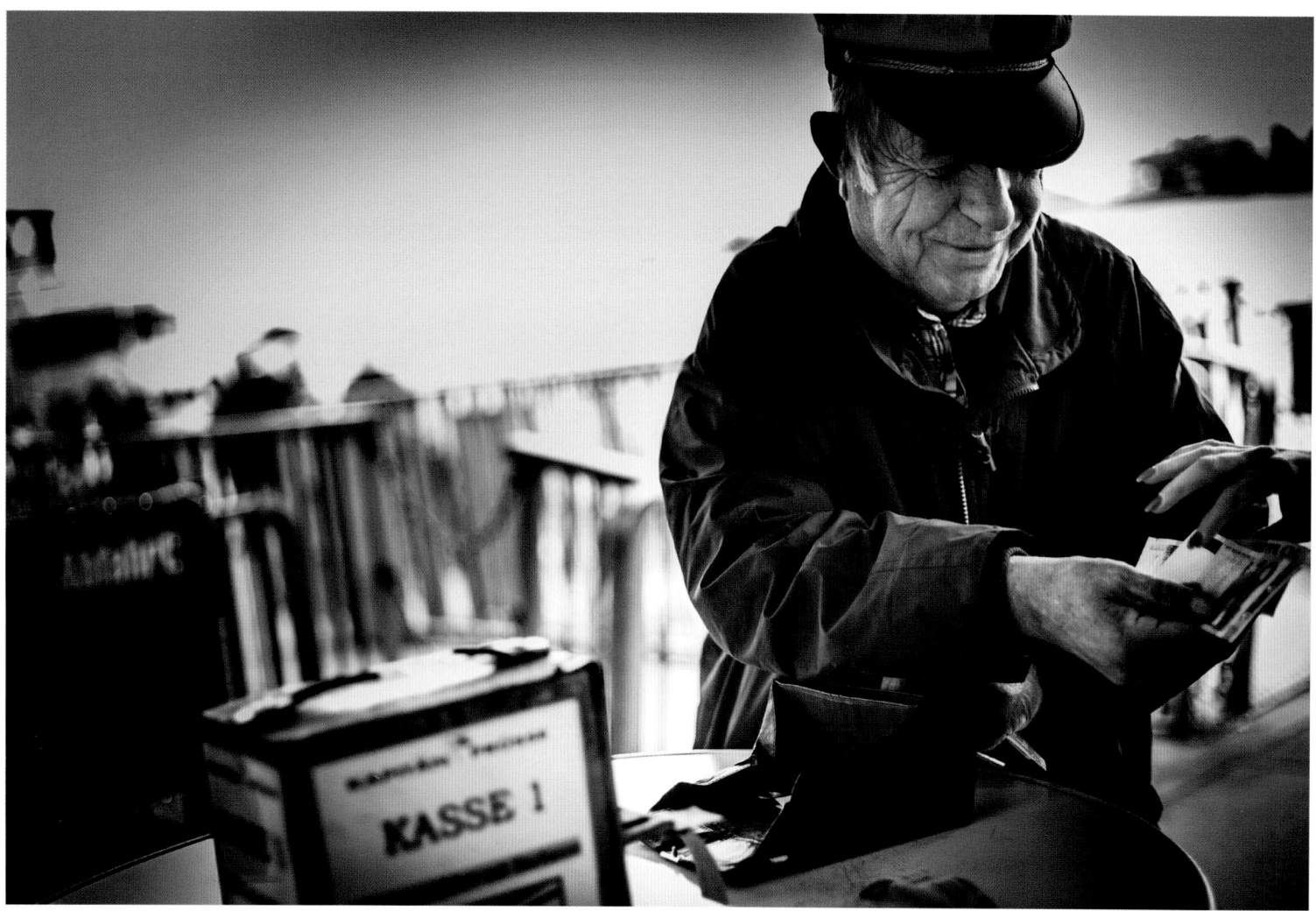

Captain Birdseye selling tickets for harbor tours. In this shot, I deliberately reduced the depth of field to obscure the distracting background, and the manicured hand of the woman buying the ticket adds an offbeat element. The overall composition doesn't follow any traditional rules.

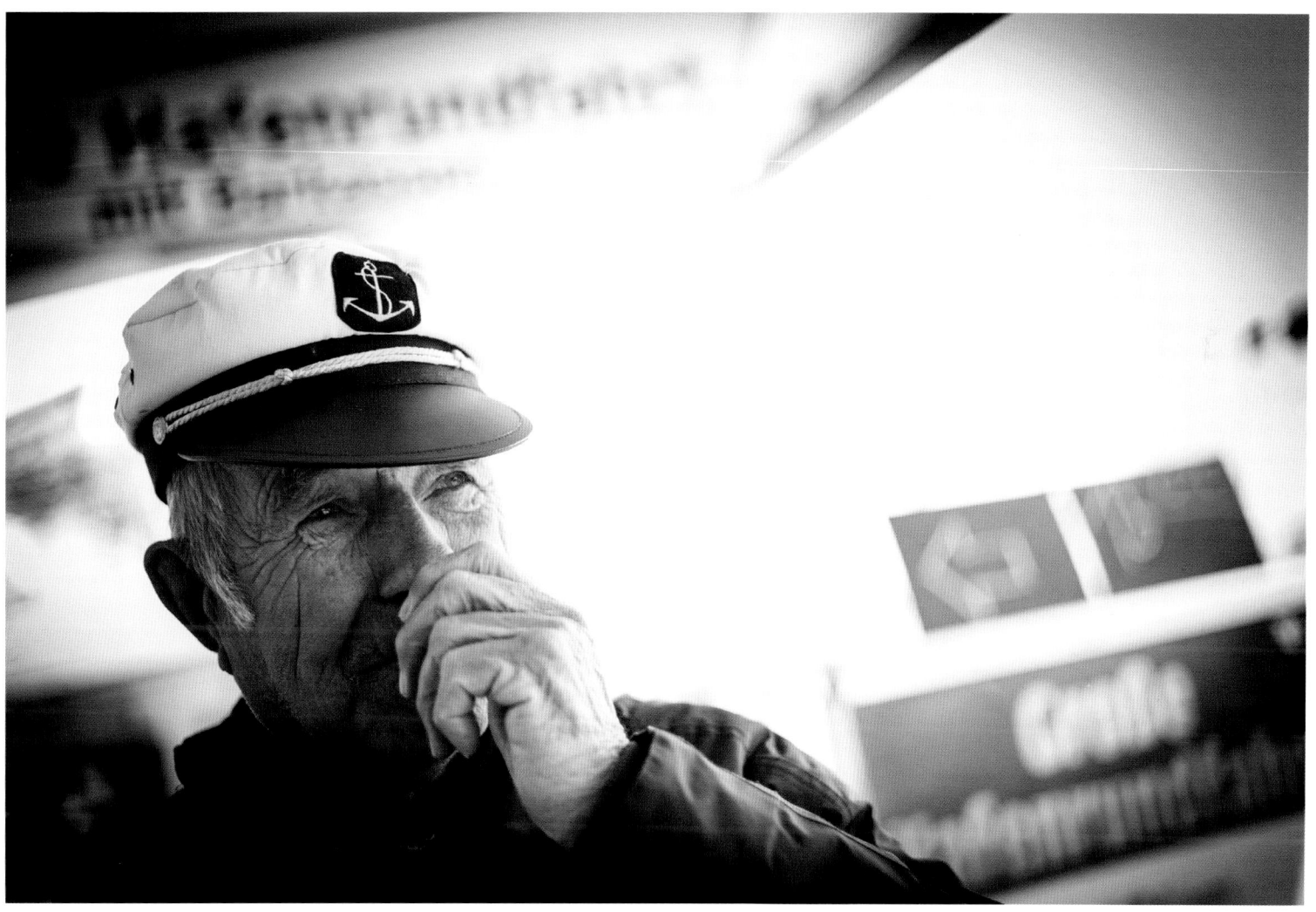

There is no reason a story shouldn't contain two images of the same person as long as they are sufficiently varied. This image combines classic composition with a wide-open aperture and a slight tilt of the camera.

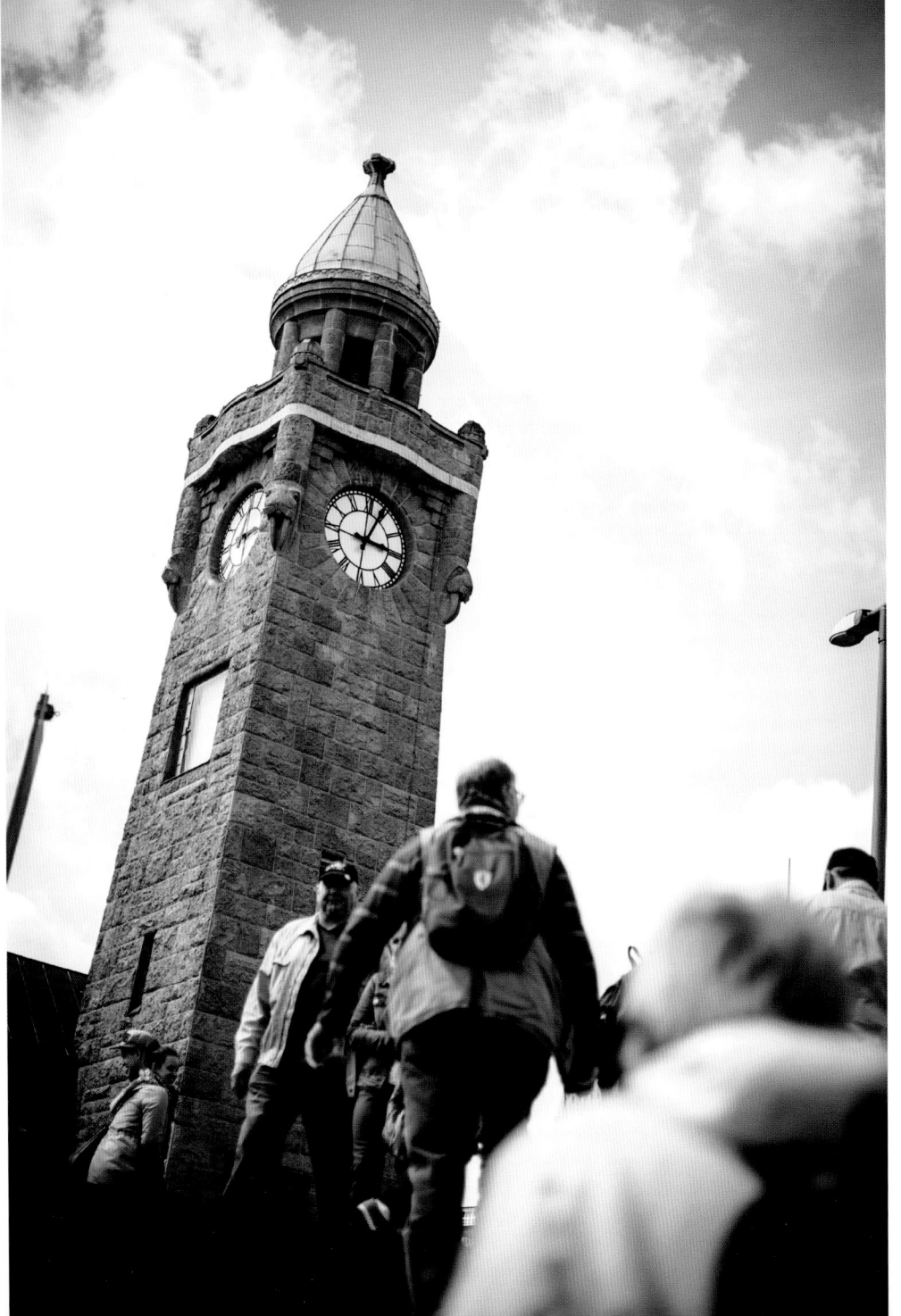

The clock tower with its flood level indicator is a tourist magnet. The foreground blur is deliberate.

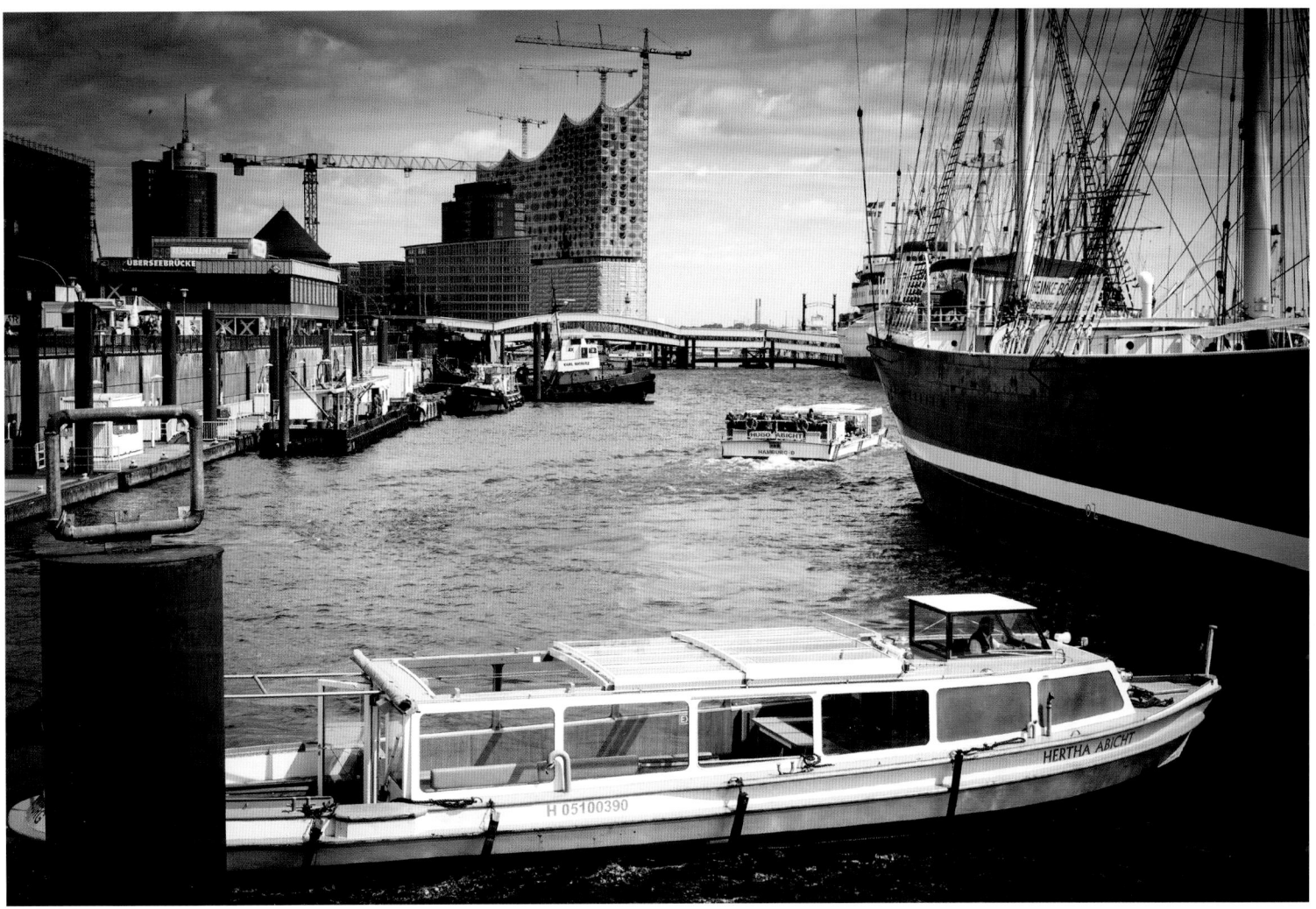

Water and boats are the lifeblood of every harbor town. This image is framed perfectly by the bollard on the left, the three-masted ship *Rickmer Rickmers* on the right, the *Hertha Abicht* in the foreground, and the pontoon bridge in the distance.

5. Without a Map, You Won't Reach Your Destination
The Importance of Planning

All you wanted was to learn a little and enjoy taking photos with your Leica, and here I come to spoil the fun with a chapter about planning.

Let me explain why good planning is essential if a photo shoot is to be successful. In the first chapter, I advised you to keep your camera ready at all times and not to let it languish in your camera bag. Carrying your Leica over your shoulder or hung around your neck enables you to react quickly, but you still need to find your subjects. After all, even a Leica doesn't have a built-in "great subject" alarm.

What is the Best Way to Find Interesting Subjects?

You can only find what you look for and if you don't know what you're looking for, you won't find anything. Even your primed Leica won't help. You need to take the time to look for a theme and develop your ideas.

Robert Capa, who was one of the founders of the Magnum agency said, "If your pictures aren't good enough, you're not close enough." I think this quote is often misinterpreted. I believe Capa was referring to psychological and emotional closeness rather than physical proximity to the subject. The intensity of a photo is all about the emotional link between the photographer and the situation being portrayed.

How Does Closeness Develop between the Photographer and the Subject?

There are many ways to approach a subject. The simplest approach is to photograph familiar people and places. My daughter, for example, doesn't even notice any more when I get out my camera and take a couple of snaps. Ever since she was born, her father has carried a camera and taken photos, and our family bond means I don't have to build a relationship with her every time I want to take a photo.

In 2013, Magnum photographer Christopher Anderson published a book called *SON*. The book portrays the relationships between Anderson, his ailing father, and his growing son. The photos contrast his father's suffering with his son's lightheartedness and the result is a poetic, multi-layered family story. It is a great example of a theme that anyone can tackle—with or without the additional sub-theme of illness.

Other photographers prefer to deal with places rather than people, such as Magnum member Alec Soth, who chose the Mississippi River and Niagara Falls as his subjects. Rather than typical travel photo books, Soth has created picture books that look behind the scenes and portray his highly personal feelings toward his subjects. Belgian photographer Stephan Vanfleteren has published several photo books about his homeland, offering a personal perspective that engenders curiosity in the viewer about the land and its people.

What Does All of This Have to Do with Planning?

Neither I nor any of the photographers I have mentioned simply left the house and started shooting. We all did our research, developed a plan, and created a certain closeness to the subject before we began to shoot.

Practically speaking, you won't have to find a theme if you find a specific person or event to photograph. It could be a child's birthday, a wedding, famous visitors in town, a car race, a portrait of an artist, your mother-in-law, or a story about the longest freeway in the country. Or maybe you could get to know the anglers at the local fishing spot or the town fire brigade. Have you spotted the difference between the professional and amateur themes here? Exactly—there is none! A professional photographer can be given an assignment of photographing a birthday, just as a hobbyist could choose to capture a personal view of a state official's visit, even if he doesn't get press accreditation (not all pros do either, by the way). It would do some newspapers good, too, if they moved away from printing the same old pictures of the same old hands being shaken.

The other way to find a theme is simply to give yourself an assignment. This can be any subject that interests you, like my "People at Polo Matches" project, for example. An assignment can be quite specific—such as events at the emergency ward at a hospital—or it can be more conceptual, like my German Angst series (chapter 3 On Assignment).

Once I have an assignment, whether one of my own or for someone else, I begin my background research. For simpler subjects, access to the Internet means I usually need my iPad or iPhone to find what I need. For complex subjects I often purchase relevant literature. I always try to learn as much as I can about the subject as well as the geography of the location so I can plan a detailed schedule. You can build a schedule around the timing of the events you will cover, the position of the sun at a climbing wall, or any other aspect of your theme.

Planning can involve photographing recurring or special events. For example, in the course of my German Angst project, I visited the Karneval (Mardi Gras) celebrations in Cologne. I had an idea of what to expect before I went, but the photos I captured exceeded my wildest hopes. By researching, I challenged Lady Luck and was rewarded with fantastic images.

A good photographer is curious and likes to engage with the people he meets along the way. If you head out with wakeful eyes, an open mind, and an idea of what you are looking for, you are sure to be rewarded with great results. If, however, you think you can casually capture an effective photo story by chance, you are likely to be disappointed. High quality photography takes hard work, both physically and psychologically, but it is also incredibly satisfying.

Photo Exercise #5

Find a theme, do background research, and draft a plan for your shoot. Consider how you can capture your subject in 10 strong images. Remember to research the physical and geographical aspects of the location, such as the position of the sun, water levels, the potential volume of traffic, and scheduled public gatherings.

My Daughter Janne

Even for a professional photographer, shooting family photos is a great way to practice. I find that watching my family and taking photos of them is really relaxing. I don't have to explain myself because they are used to me snapping away and I can simply get on with doing what I like to do.

I began taking photos of my daughter before her umbilical cord was cut (and I am still amazed that I managed to capture those images with my M6, which required me to set exposure and focus manually and wind the film by hand). Janne has been used to me pointing a camera at her from very early on!

Over the years, I have shot photos of her using color and black-and-white film and I have converted my digital images using the Lightroom Creamtone preset and dialed the colors down to almost nothing. In other words, I have tried just about everything to get the images right. The results always incorporate how I felt at the time. As I looked through my images while choosing the photos for this book, I realized that I often tried new ideas in photos of Janne. I usually test a new camera and new shooting techniques at home and I always show the results to my family first.

My work over the last 12 years also documents developments in photographic technology, which means that between 2004 and 2008, I didn't take any pictures of my daughter using a Leica. I haven't shot on film since 2004. Leica was

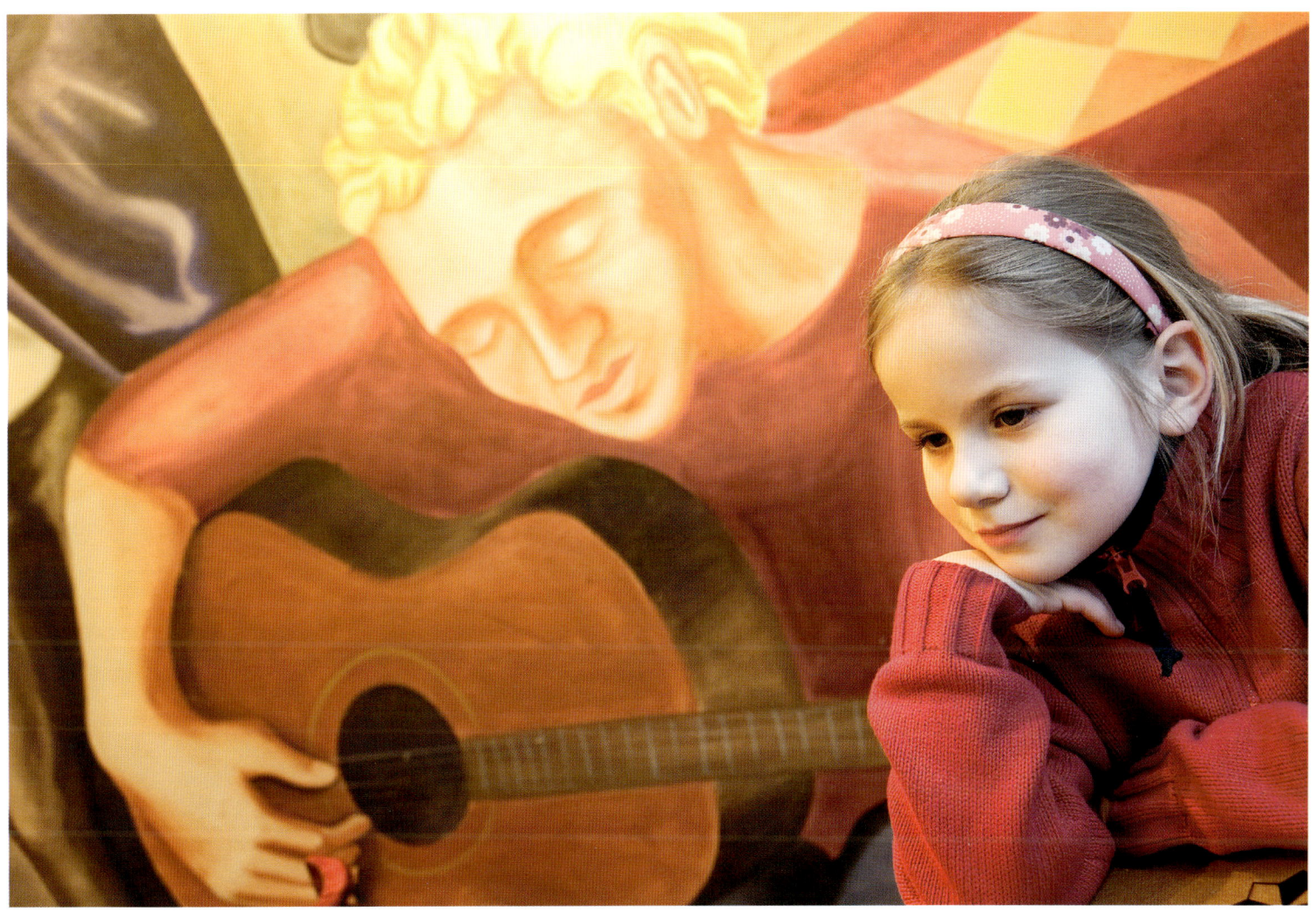

This color image is monochromatic, and the foreground and background merge almost imperceptibly. The image looks three-dimensional and the strong diagonal composition adds tension. Leica M8, 24mm

slow to adapt to digital photography, so I used other digital camera systems until Leica caught up.

This long-term project shows that reportage can follow a process over an indefinite period of time—in this case, my daughter's childhood. The most important aspect of this type of project is to stick with it. It's difficult to judge the importance of individual events at the time, so you just continue to collect material.

And by the way, photographing the same person over a period of years is a great way to hone your portrait photography skills.

All the pictures in this book were captured using Leica M cameras. Because there is a significant portion of Janne's life that was captured using cameras other than Leicas, you will notice that her younger years are not represented here.

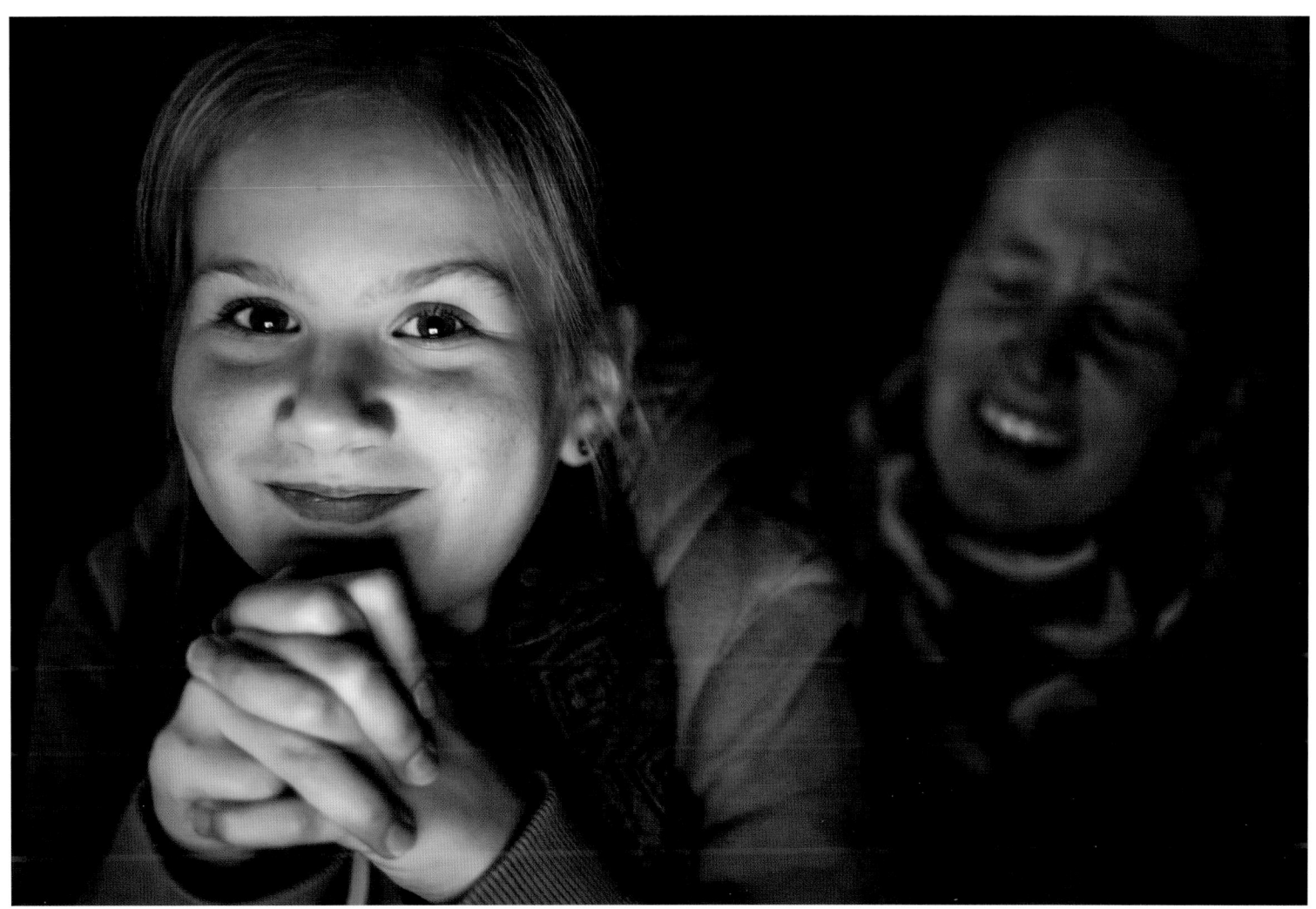

Mother and daughter having fun together. A lateral spotlight provided the modest lighting and produced the reflections in Janne's eyes. I reduced color saturation in Lightroom. M9, f/2, 1/15 s, ISO 640, 50mm, handheld

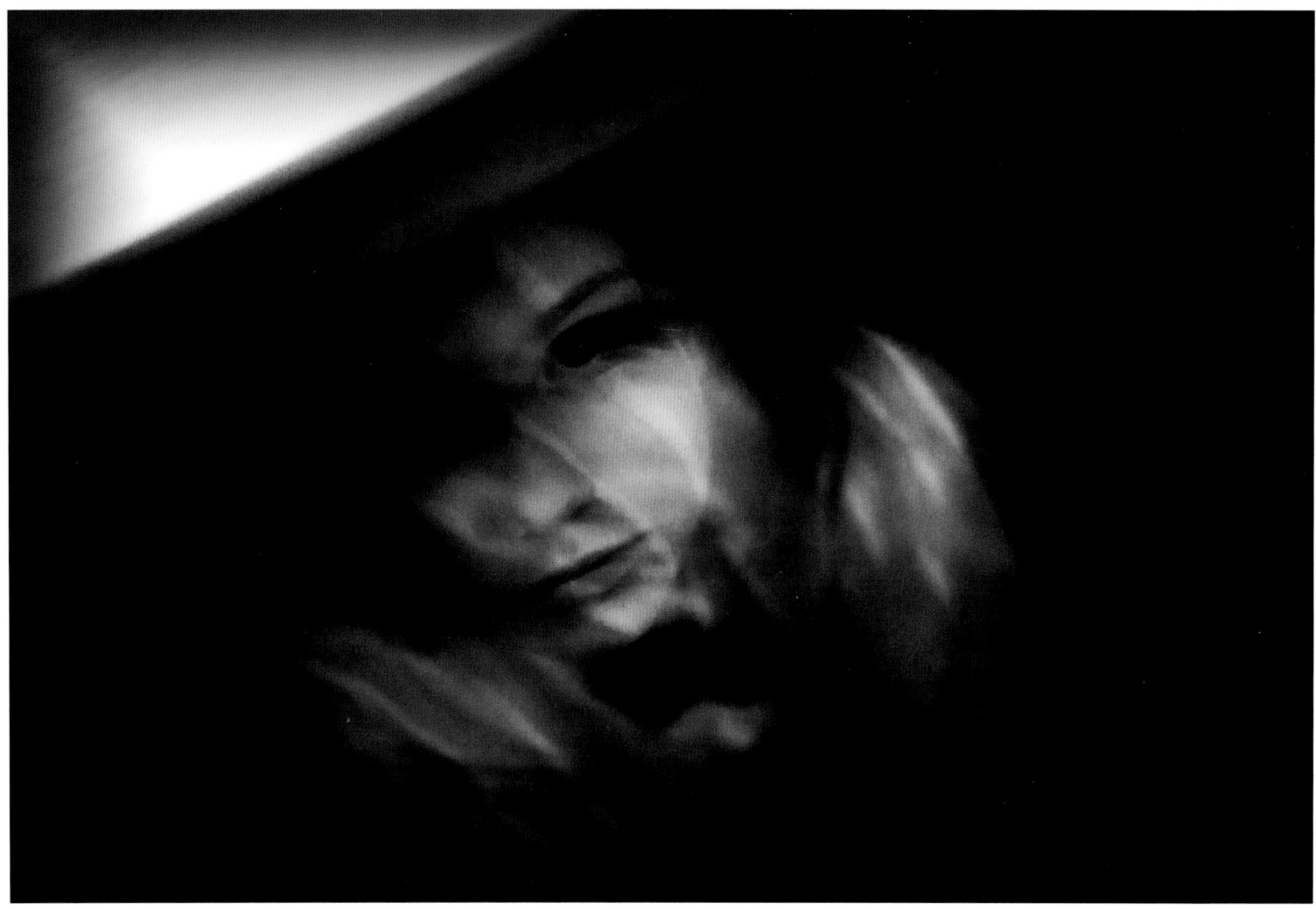

Janne under the table, because that's where kids sometimes hang out. The streaked light came from a wall lamp and the overall effect was created using a long exposure. Leica M9, 1/8 s, 50mm

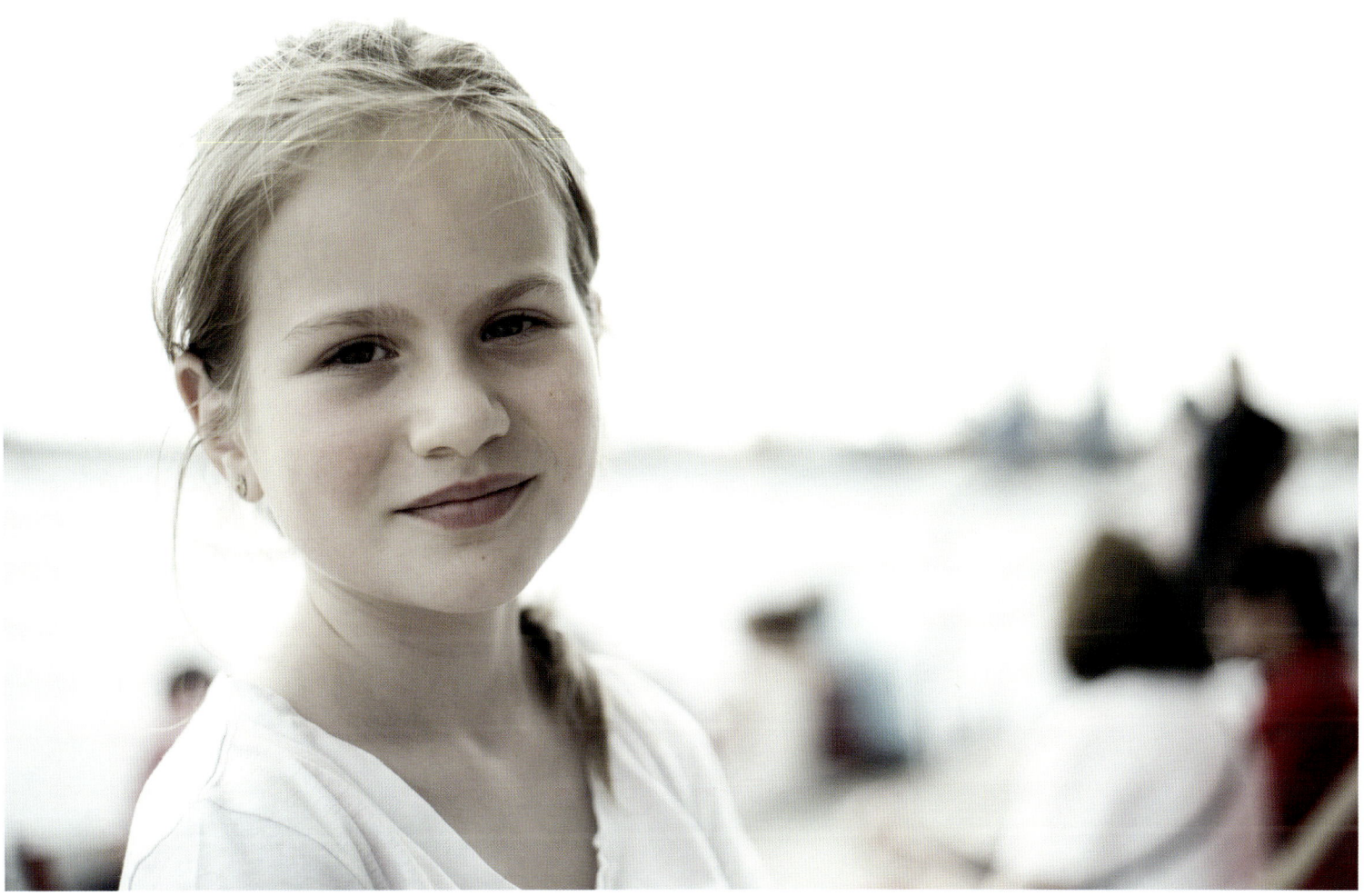

Deliberate overexposure of about one full f-stop. Captured using a 50mm Summicron at maximum aperture, this shot has wonderful background blur. I also used a neutral density filter to enable me to shoot with the aperture wide open. I reduced the intensity of the colors later in Lightroom.

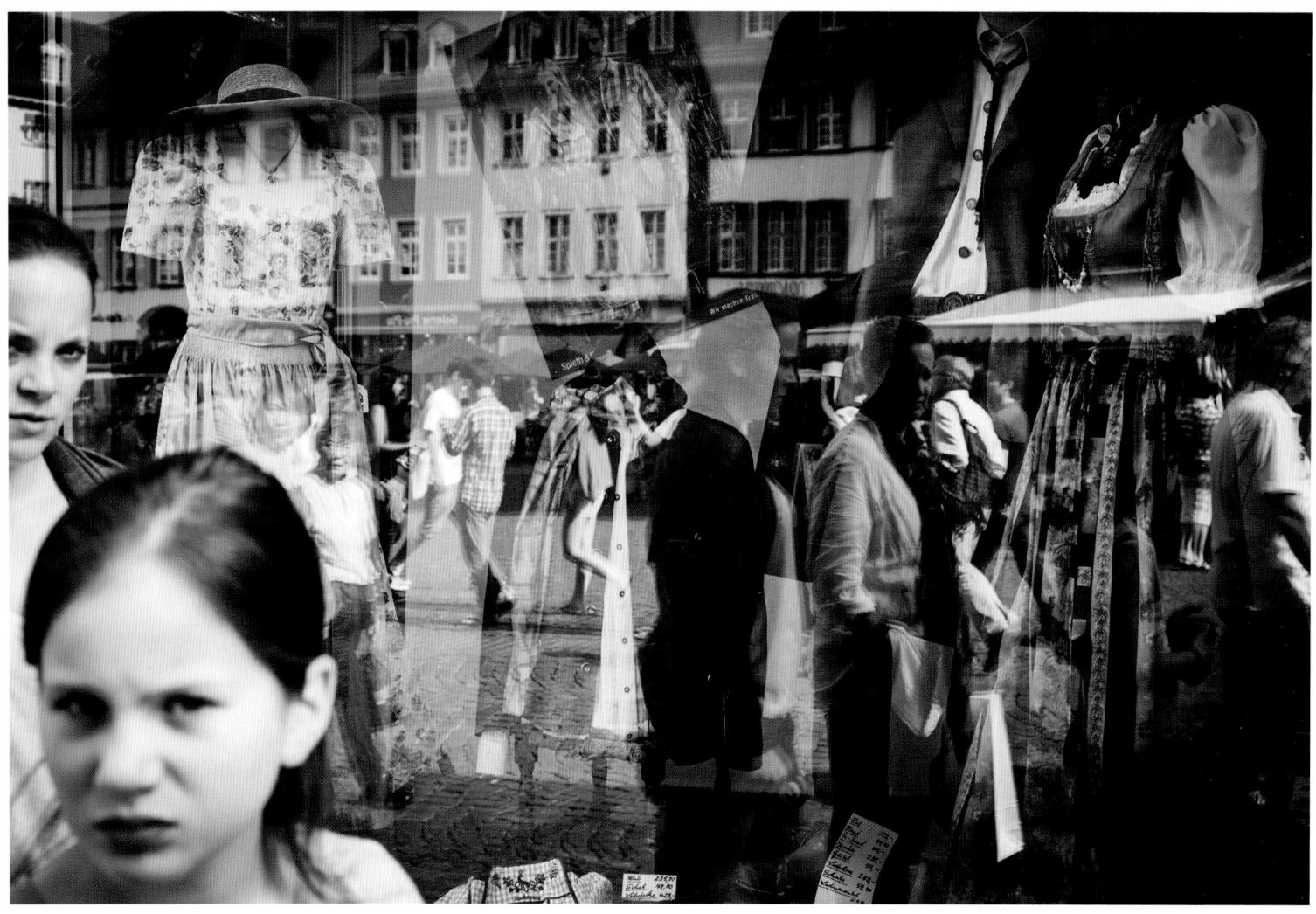

Janne visiting her older sister in Heidelberg. The houses reflected in the shop window and Janne's critical expression are the main features. The girls were moving toward me so I focused deliberately on the reflections behind them.

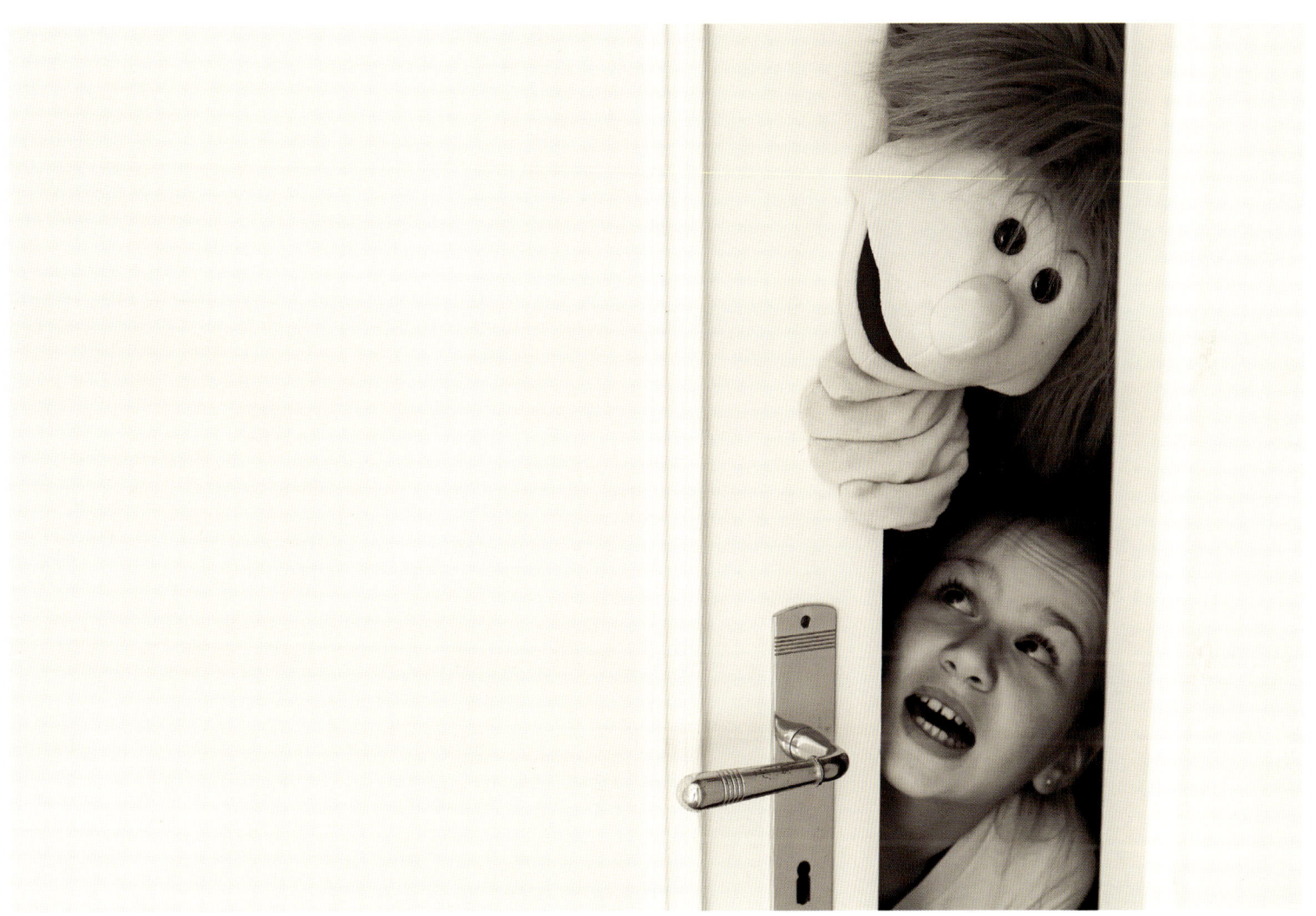

Janne and Kalle in a posed image I shot for our annual family calendar

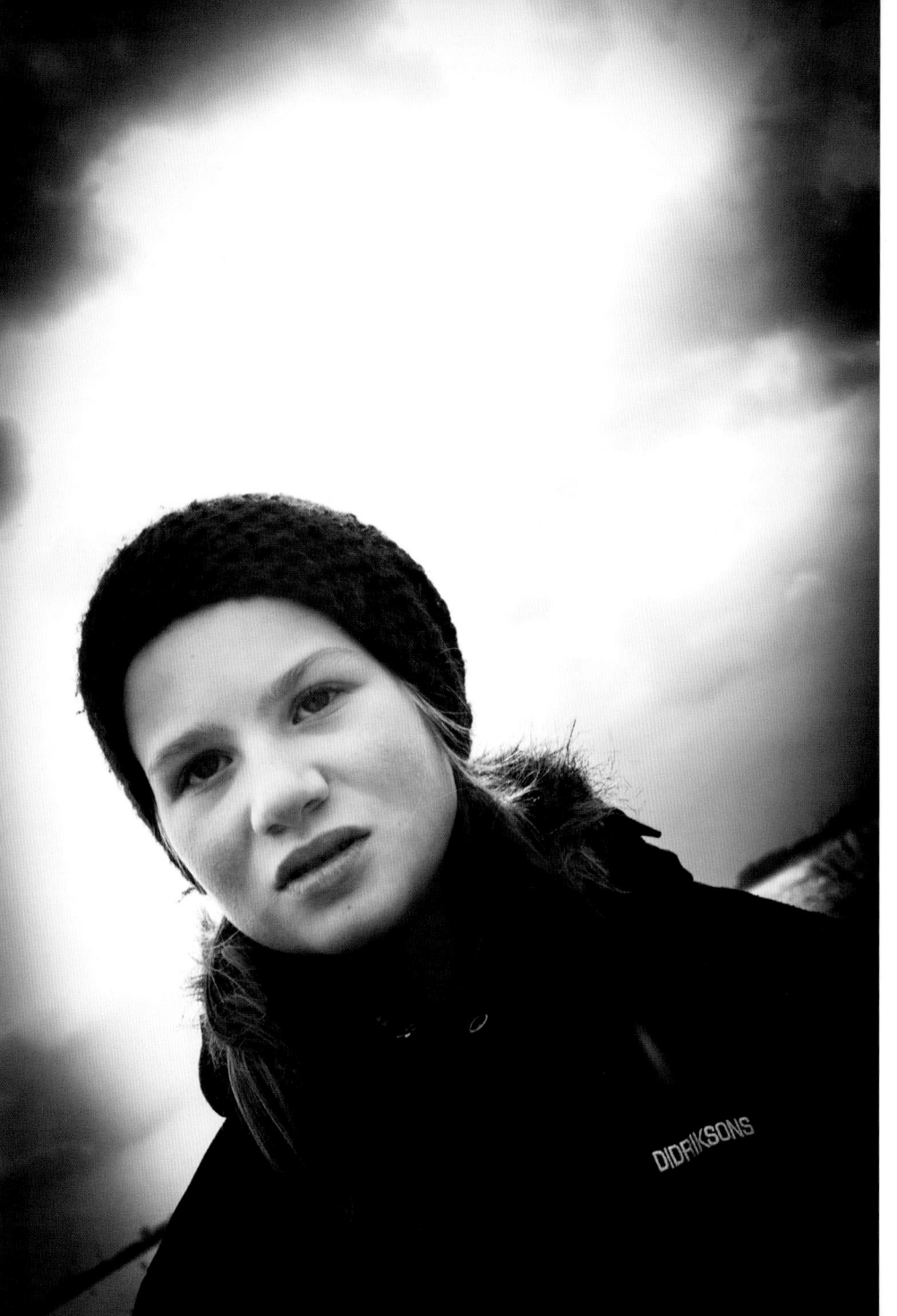

I love the combined effect of Janne's expression and the clouds in the background. I tilted the camera deliberately and placed the subject off-center to complete the composition.

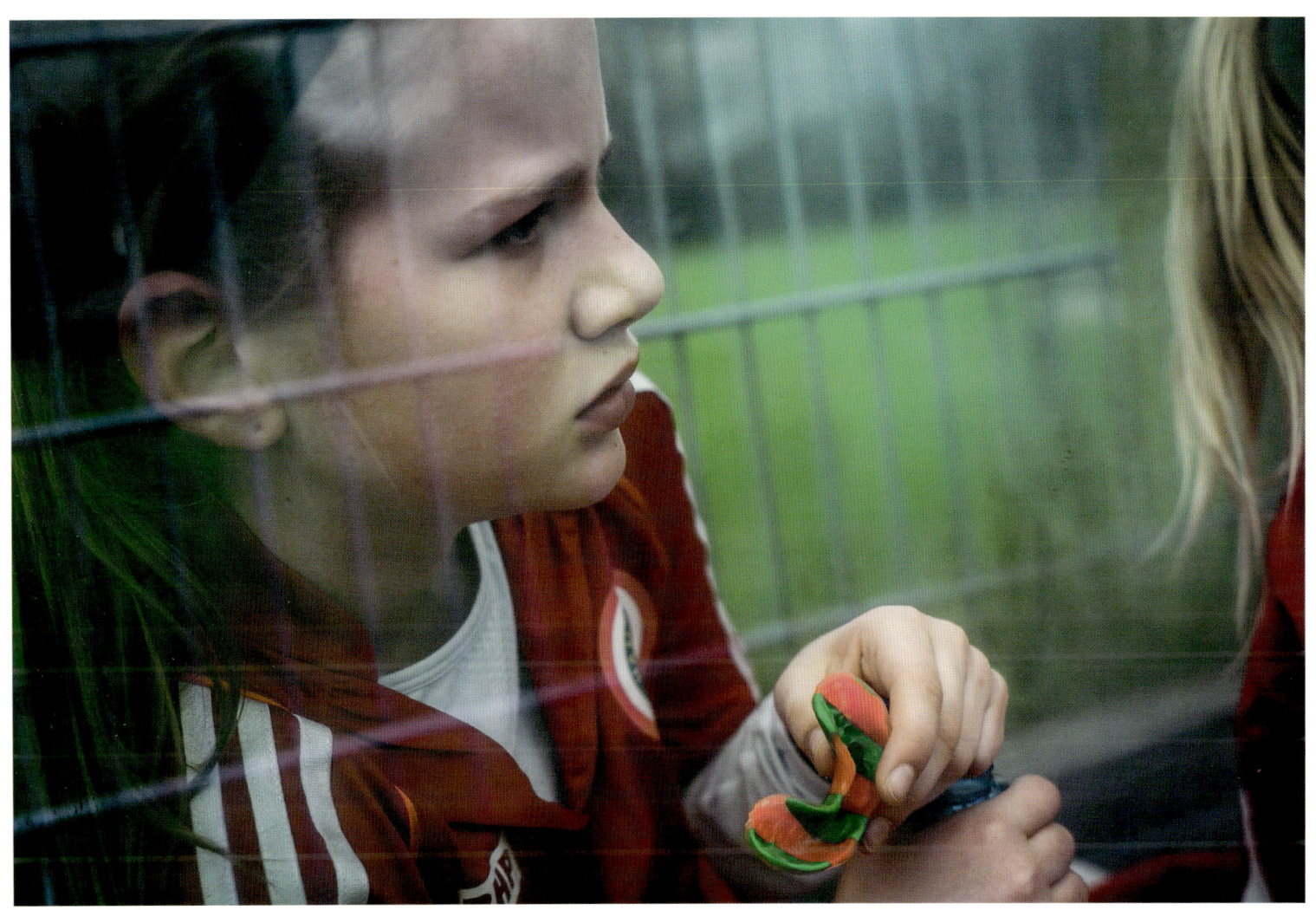

At a hockey tournament. This shot was captured through the Plexiglas of the trainer's dugout. The reflected wire mesh gives the image added depth.

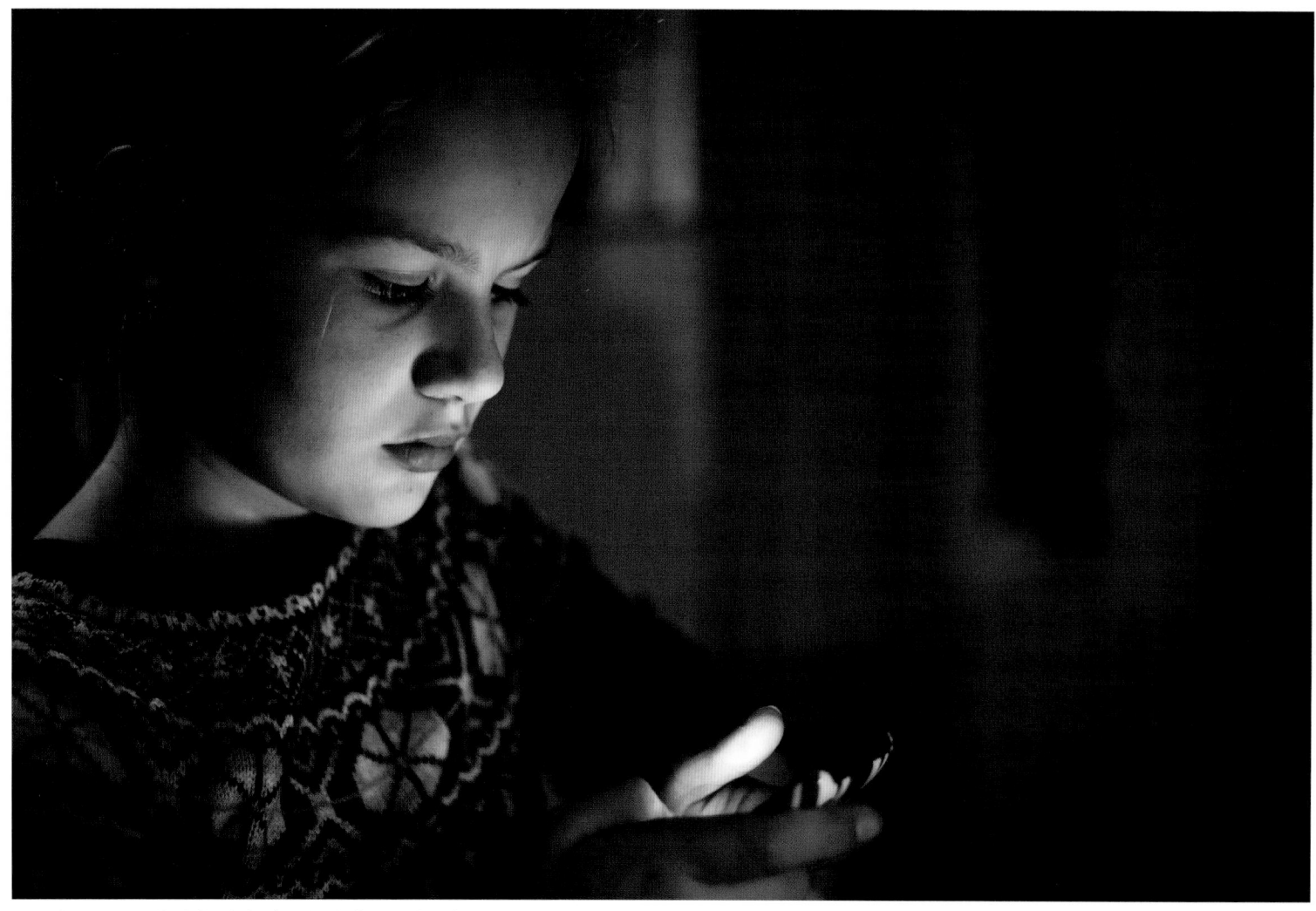

An iPhone provided the light for this left-weighted composition. I desaturated the colors in Lightroom.

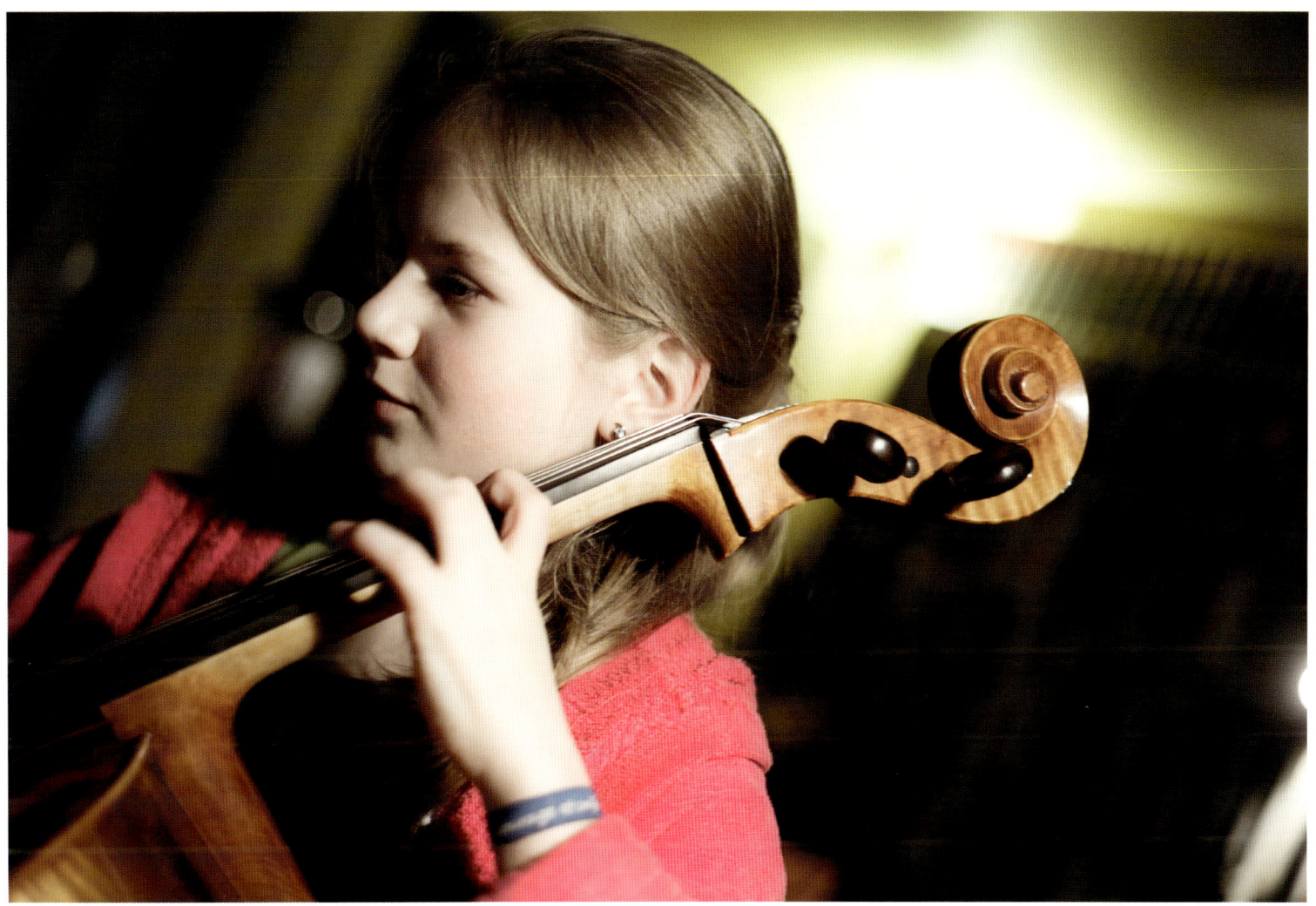

An evening mood captured in artificial light. The shallow depth of field produced by the wide aperture provides a clean background.

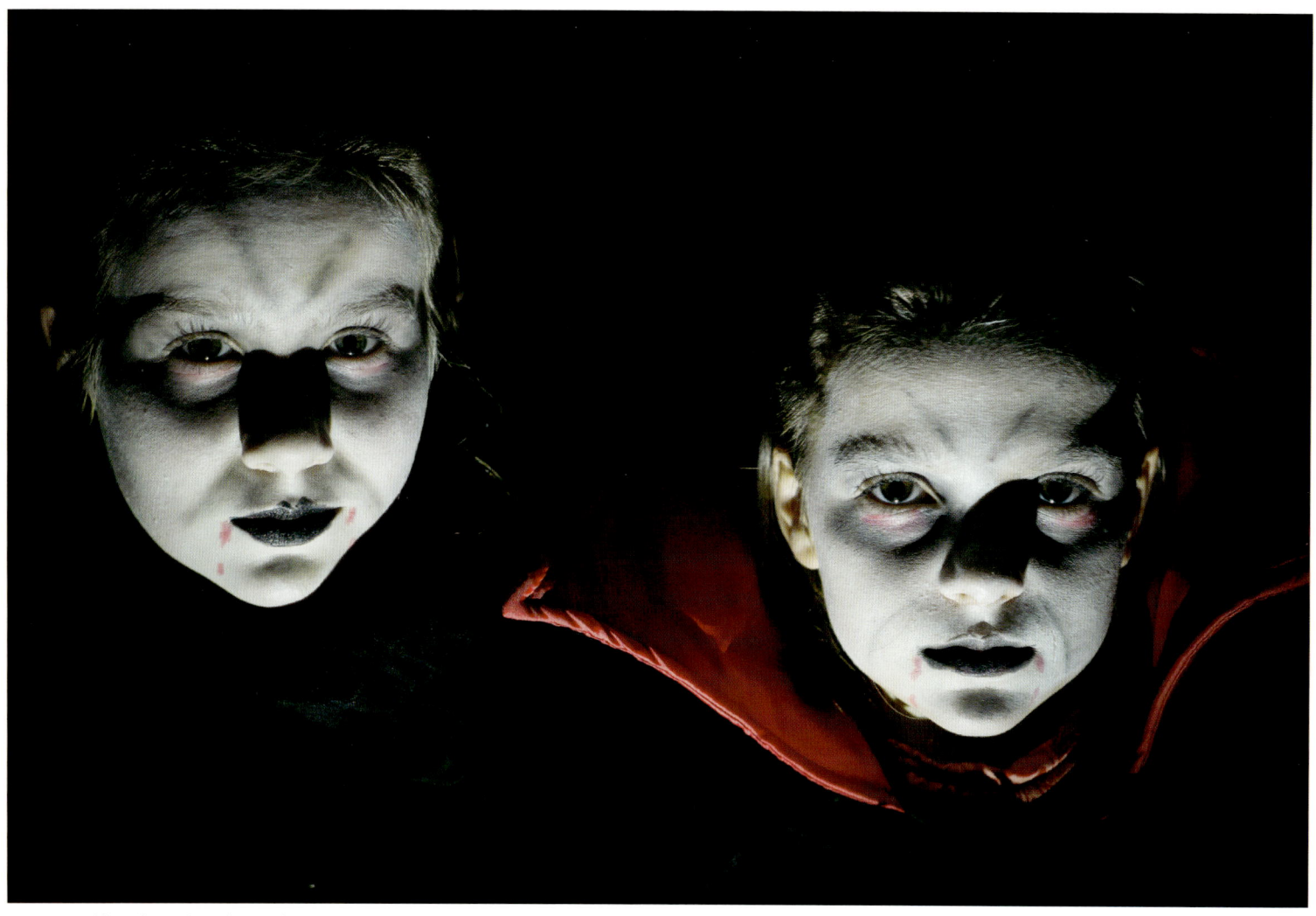

Janne and her friend Carlotta during Halloween. The light came from an LED flashlight pointed upward from waist height.
Leica M9, f/4, 1/30 s, ISO 1000, 50mm

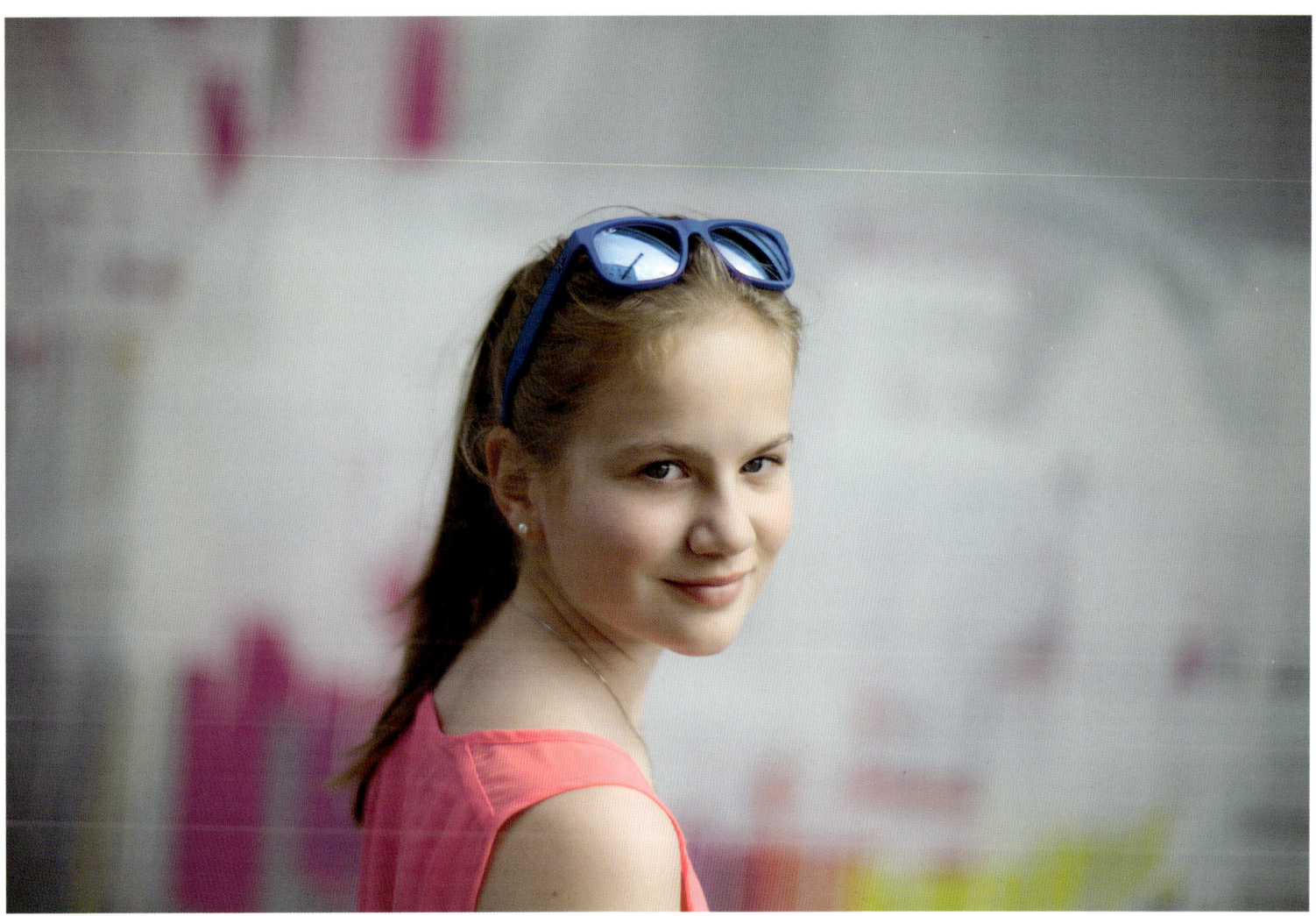

The prominent colors in this picture are white and pink, making the contrasting blue sunglasses an important element. The picture seems to be nearly three-dimensional due to the narrow field of depth. Leica M9 with a Voigtlander Nokton 1.2/35 mm at 2.0 with an ND Filter.

6. Making Mistakes
The Benefits and Drawbacks of Rules

Do textbooks and rules make sense in a photographic context? If you want to do arithmetic accurately, you have to stick to the rules. If you want to take great photos, you have to know the rules too, but you can ignore them if you want. Many photography textbooks aim to help us avoid making common mistakes and talk about the "right" composition, "correct" exposure and "ideal" shutter speeds.

I think terms like "right" and "wrong" simply don't apply when it comes to taking photos. Photography is a creative pursuit. Anyone involved in creating photographs for anything other than purely documentary purposes doesn't need to enslave themselves to rules and should instead concentrate on packing their images with emotion. But don't get me wrong—an unintentionally blurred image is substandard regardless of how creatively you shoot it. On the other hand, deliberate motion blur can be an effective stylistic device. Let's take a look at some of the more generally accepted "rules" of photography.

Image Composition

Your subject doesn't have to be positioned in the center of the frame just because that's where you focused or because it was the most obvious composition. On the other hand, positioning a portrait subject in the center of the frame can make the shot more interesting. Generally speaking, the subject can be positioned anywhere within the frame.

The rule of thirds is a compositional tool that is popular among photographers and painters. The idea is that you draw imaginary lines through the frame to divide it into nine identically sized areas (or thirds, vertically and horizontally) and then place the subject at an intersection of two of the lines. This is a simple way to create compositions that differentiate clearly between the foreground and the background. However, it is not a guaranteed recipe for great images and there are many photos that leave a positive impression on the viewer precisely because they weren't composed using strict guidelines.

A sharp background subject can be framed by a blurred foreground, just as blur and depth-of-field effects are highly versatile tools for enhancing a composition. Nevertheless, images that are pin sharp from the near foreground all the way to infinity can be appealing, too if the overall composition is well thought out.

Horizons don't have to be level but, if you do use a slanted horizon, make sure that it is part of the overall composition; otherwise, it will simply look like you were careless.

As you can see, composition alone gives you a vast range of options, and the best way to find out what works is to try out your own variations. But don't make the mistake of trying to cram all of your ideas into a single story. Not every style suits every job. Remember: less is sometimes more.

Light

Generally speaking, light comes either from the sun (i.e., daylight) or from an artificial source. Both types have variable brightnesses (i.e., intensity) and temperatures (i.e., color).

Morning daylight has a blue hue, changing to white toward midday and to orange/red at sunset before it once again takes on a blue tone at dusk. The intensity of daylight varies during the day, too, and is brightest at midday. Clouds reduce the sun's intensity, and shaded daylight tends toward blue. Fashion photographers often use the soft, warm look of early morning or late evening sunlight, which is a tip that you will find in a lot of books on photography.

However, if you know what you are doing, you can also use the cold, hard midday sun to produce excellent photos. This is another aspect of the image capture process that underscores the need to plan in advance the effect you want to produce.

In the realm of artificial light, neon light has a green shimmer while incandescent light bulbs produce an orange glow. Advertising billboards can bathe entire streets in color. The myriad options offered by different sources of light have their proponents and detractors and many textbooks advise you to simply cancel out the effects of artificial light by using artificial daylight (i.e., flash). I like the tension and authenticity that different light sources provide, although I sometimes use flash. I always try to consider the effect I want to achieve before I release the shutter, which often means I will try out several variants for a single shot. This takes us nicely on to our next subject…

Exposure

Is there such a thing as "correct" exposure? You can use a handheld exposure meter to determine exposure parameters that, objectively speaking, will produce a correct exposure. The question here is whether using these values produces an interesting image. Images produced using standard criteria won't upset the viewer, but they won't win any prizes either. If, on the other hand, you decide to expose for highlight or shadow detail, you are sure to produce more engaging results. The selective metering capability built into many Leica models provides you with a great tool for doing just that.

Textbooks often recommend that you prevent unwanted camera shake by using the shortest possible shutter speed, and that you avoid potential focusing errors by stopping the aperture down. This advice is fine if you want to avoid taking risks, but if you do shoot this way, you don't need a Leica with its excellent lenses. Go ahead and test your limits and those of your camera. Think about how a shot will turn out if you pan the camera during the exposure. Add motion blur or use the selective focus effects offered by wide apertures. Trying new things will mean that you produce more reject material, but that is to be expected. If you break with tradition, your work is sure to gain more attention.

Going into a lot of detail on flash is beyond the scope of this book, but there are still a couple of things I'd like to say on the subject. You can use flash as a main or fill-in light, and you can apply it directly or indirectly. The more direct the flash, the harder the light it produces, so mounting a flash on your camera's accessory shoe and pointing it straight at the subject will produce stark-looking results. The alternative is to bounce your flash off a wall, ceiling, or a reflector, which makes the light reaching the subject much softer. Both approaches can be used creatively.

If you want to use flash as a fill light, you need to meter exposure for the ambient light (whether you are shooting indoors or out) and then add a dab of flash to supplement it. If, on the other hand, you are using flash as your main light, you can meter for your subject and leave the background as underexposed as you like.

Reflectors are another simple tool for controlling the mood of the lighting in an image and are especially useful in portrait shots.

ISO Sensitivity

Images captured using high-sensitivity film or high ISO values usually show more grain or digital noise than ones shot at lower sensitivities. Textbooks often classify noise and grain as errors that are to be avoided, whereas I like to use these effects creatively.

The point of this chapter is to remind you that you need to know the rules in order to break them. If you don't know why your camera reacts the way it does, you will end up being controlled by technology when you should be using technology to control the results.

What you need: your Leica M with a 35mm or 50mm lens and a person you know well for your subject.

Capture a portrait photo without thinking too hard about how you would normally approach the task.

Now alter your framing and shoot some more. It doesn't matter if your subject is positioned at the edge

of the frame or even halfway out of it—go ahead and experiment. Continue the exercise with your sub-

ject positioned in partial shadow and try using different exposure parameters. Try out as many different

options as possible.

On Assignment
At the Polo Club

While I was still a student, the *Hamburger Abendblatt* (Hamburg Evening News) commissioned me to photograph some celebrities at the polo club in the Klein Flottbek district of Hamburg. This is really a tennis and hockey club, but there is a polo field nearby where tournaments are occasionally held.

Journalists generally prefer to spend their free time at home, so weekend jobs like this are usually finished quite quickly. However, I found the fast-moving and often dangerous game of polo fascinating to watch, so I went back the following day equipped with my SLR and a telephoto lens.

In the years that followed, I spent many a weekend at the polo field. My sports shots weren't bad, but they were no match to the ones taken by the real pros in Argentina—the

light in Hamburg isn't as dramatic and the players are not in the same class as their South American counterparts. Additionally, I found that although they were prepared to spend five-figure sums on traveling, taking care of their ponies, and taking part in a tournament, the players weren't at all interested in spending money on photographs of themselves in action.

I began to wonder how I could successfully portray this highly paradoxical sport. I already had my fill of telephoto sports shots, so once again I turned to a Leica: back then my new M8 with its 35mm lens. I tried out all sorts of exposures and experimented with toning my images, but I wasn't happy with the results.

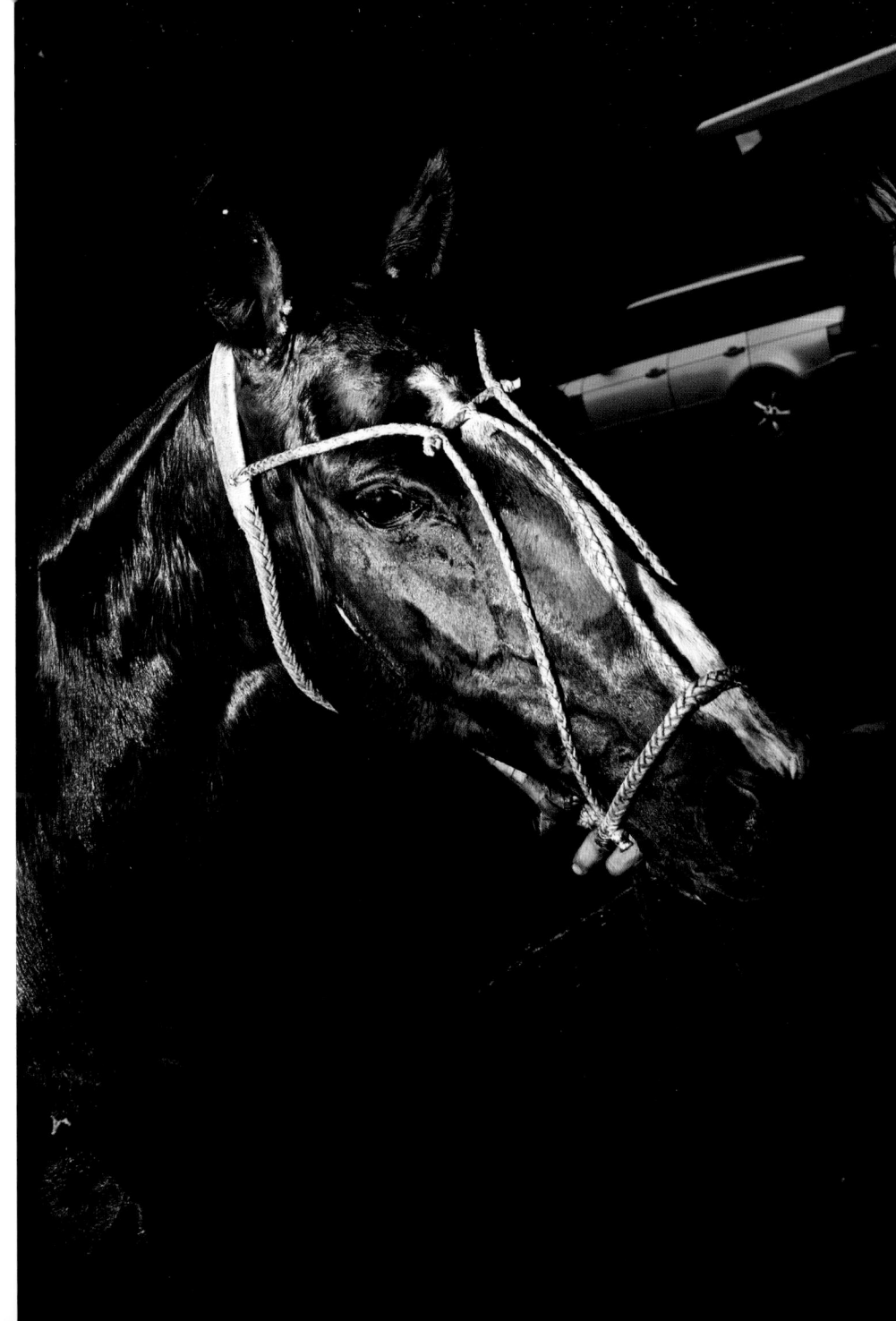

The ponies weren't bothered by my flash. Note that only bright objects in the background show up, while some of the dark areas show no detail at all.

Around the same time, I did a job for *Stern* magazine in which I increased the drama in the pictures by using daylight flash combined with heavily underexposed backgrounds and this was the technique I decided to use for my polo project.

I dug out my powerful old Quantum flashgun, acquired an adapter for its sync cable, and purchased a neutral density filter to reduce the amount of incidental light reaching the sensor. This enabled me to shoot at the shortest available flash sync speed with my lens stopped down. I metered for the ambient daylight and underexposed as much as possible. The limiting factor was the maximum output of my flash, which had to compensate for the deliberate underexposure. I set the flash to full power and adjusted exposure as necessary using the aperture. To save me having to fumble around too much with focus, I set the lens to a distance of three meters, while the stopped-down aperture took care of sharpness. I wanted to capture shots with the main light coming from a variety of directions, so I decided not to attach my flash to the camera and instead began to practice holding the camera in one hand while I pointed the flash with the other. In spite of the strong flash and my fairly bulky setup, many of the people I photographed didn't seem to notice me.

The images I captured ended up in an exhibition and a small book, and I use them on my business cards. I had a lot of fun with this project and even earned some money in the bargain.

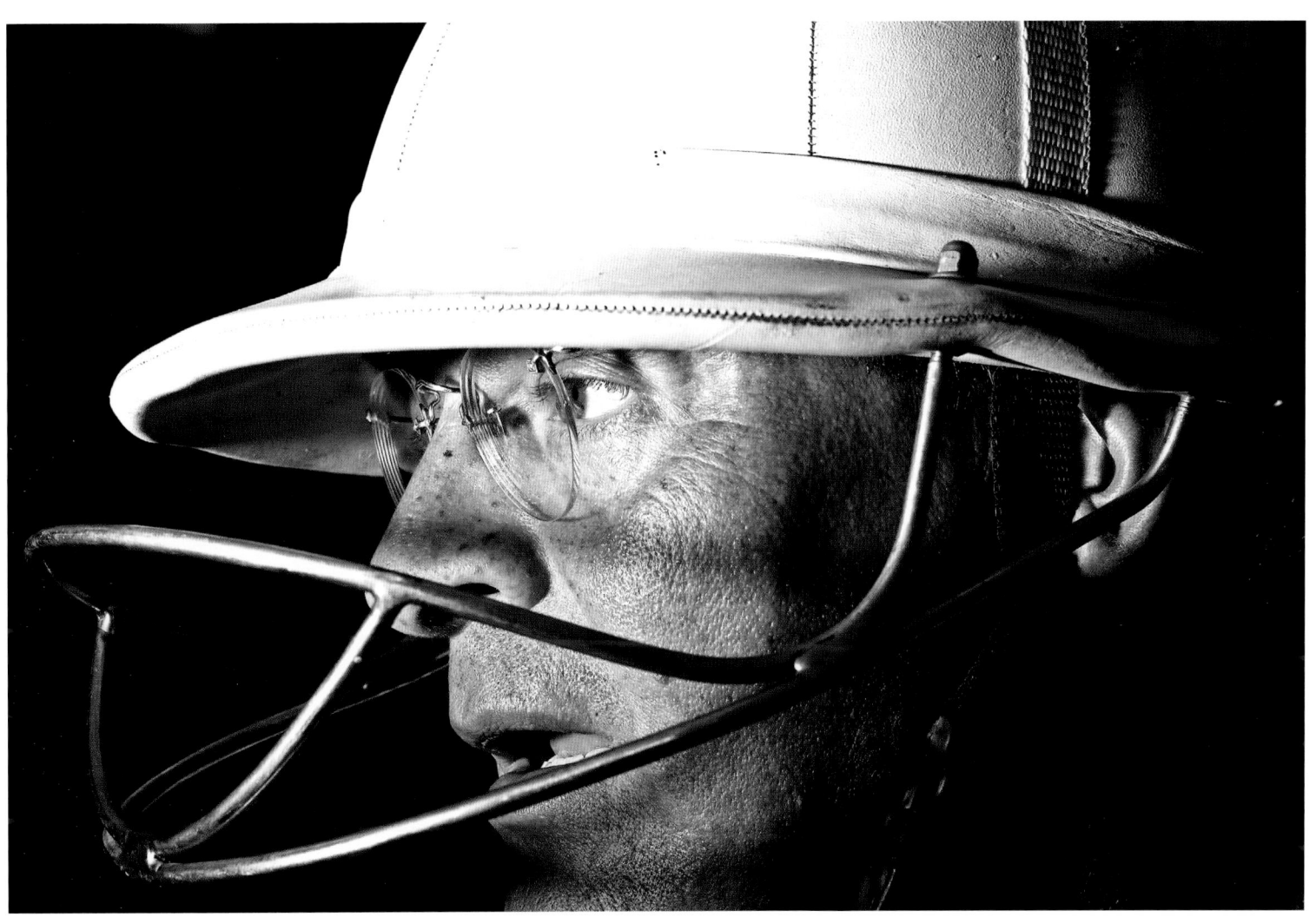

Portrait of a polo player. This shot uses great depth of field and frontal lighting combined with heavy underexposure that completely darkens the background.

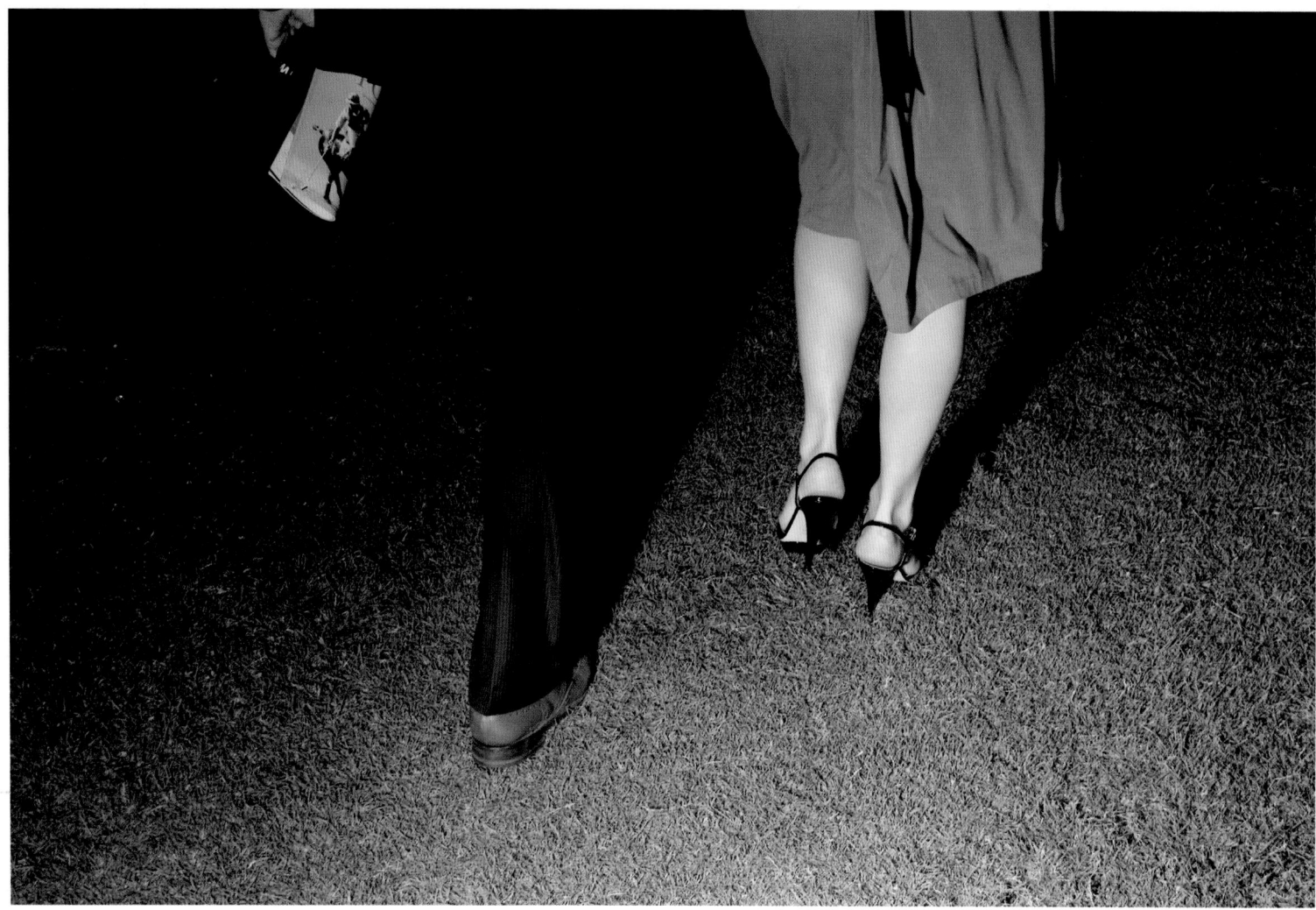

The booklet on the left is the crucial detail that transforms this into an enticing image

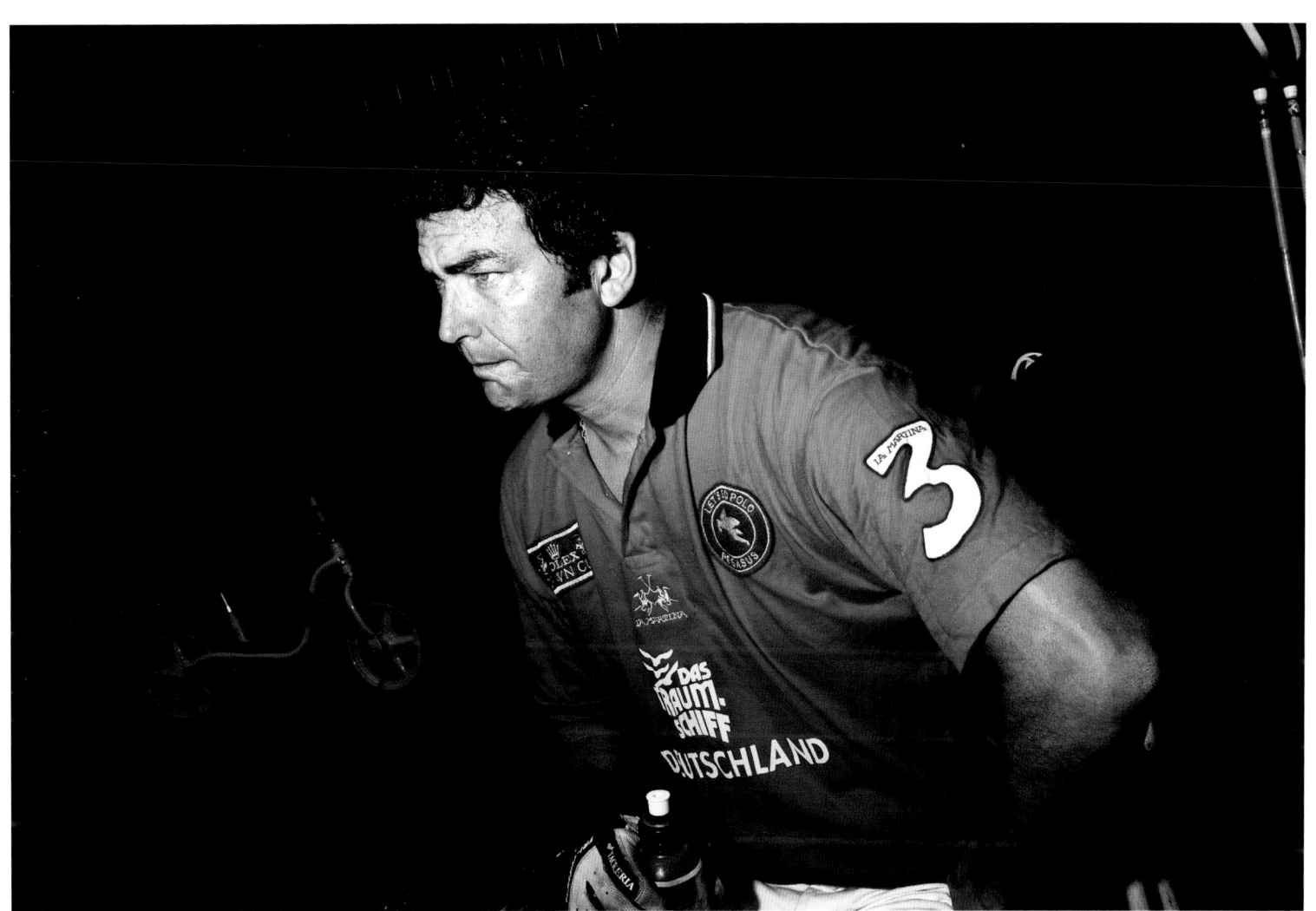

Polo player and child's scooter

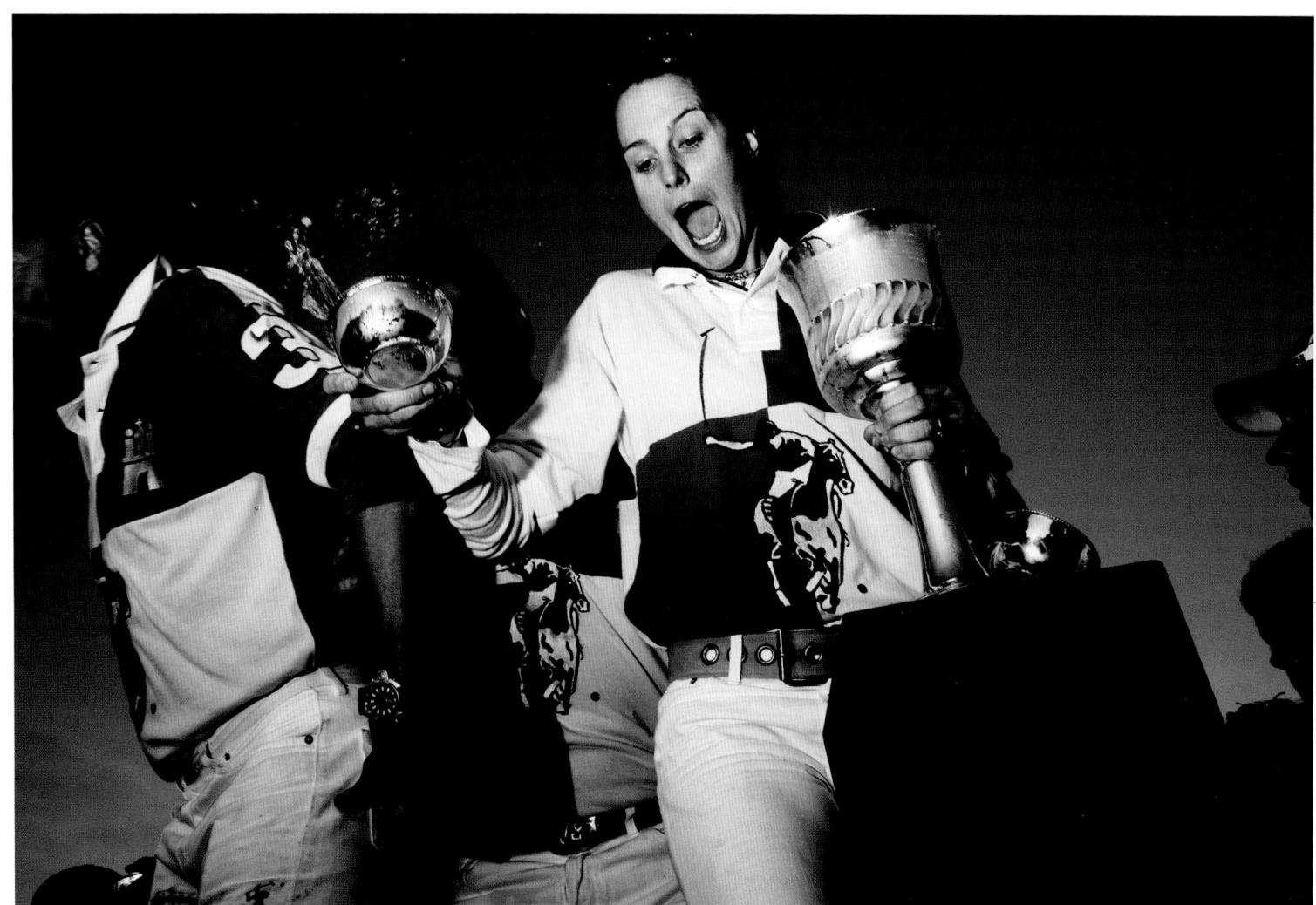

And the winner is…

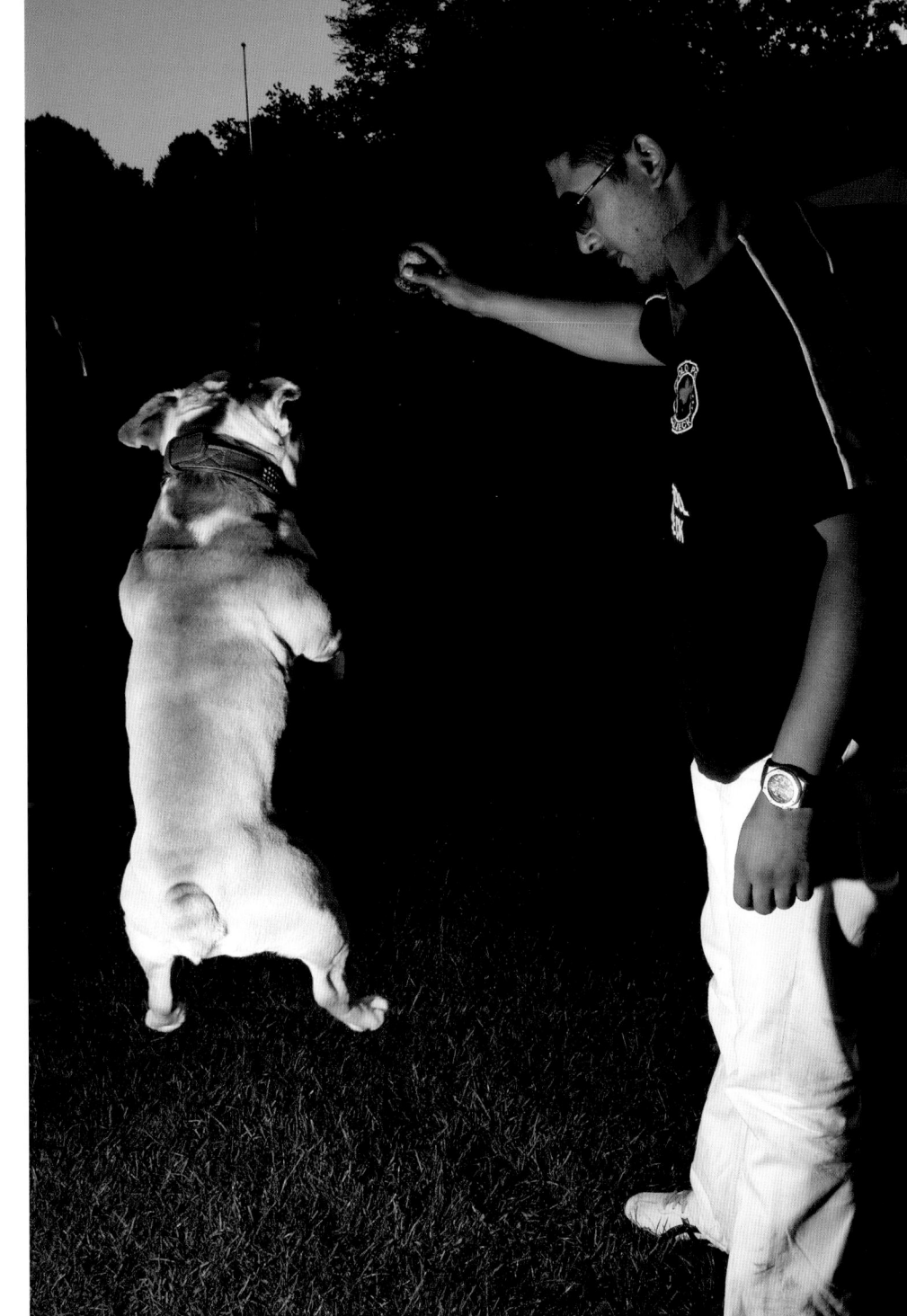

The ultra-short duration of the
flash produced a wonderful
moment frozen in time

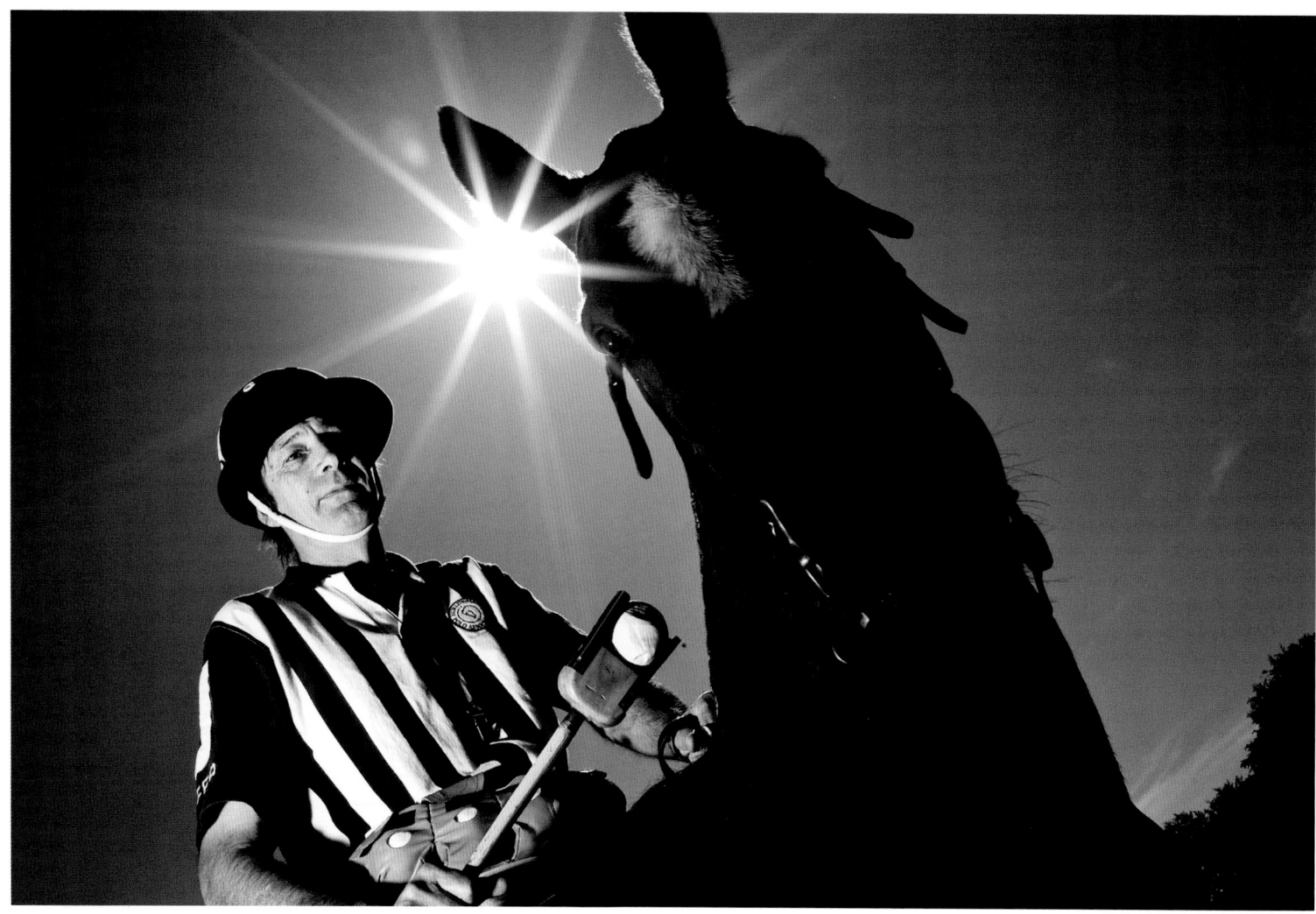

Using fill flash as a creative counterpoint to strong backlight

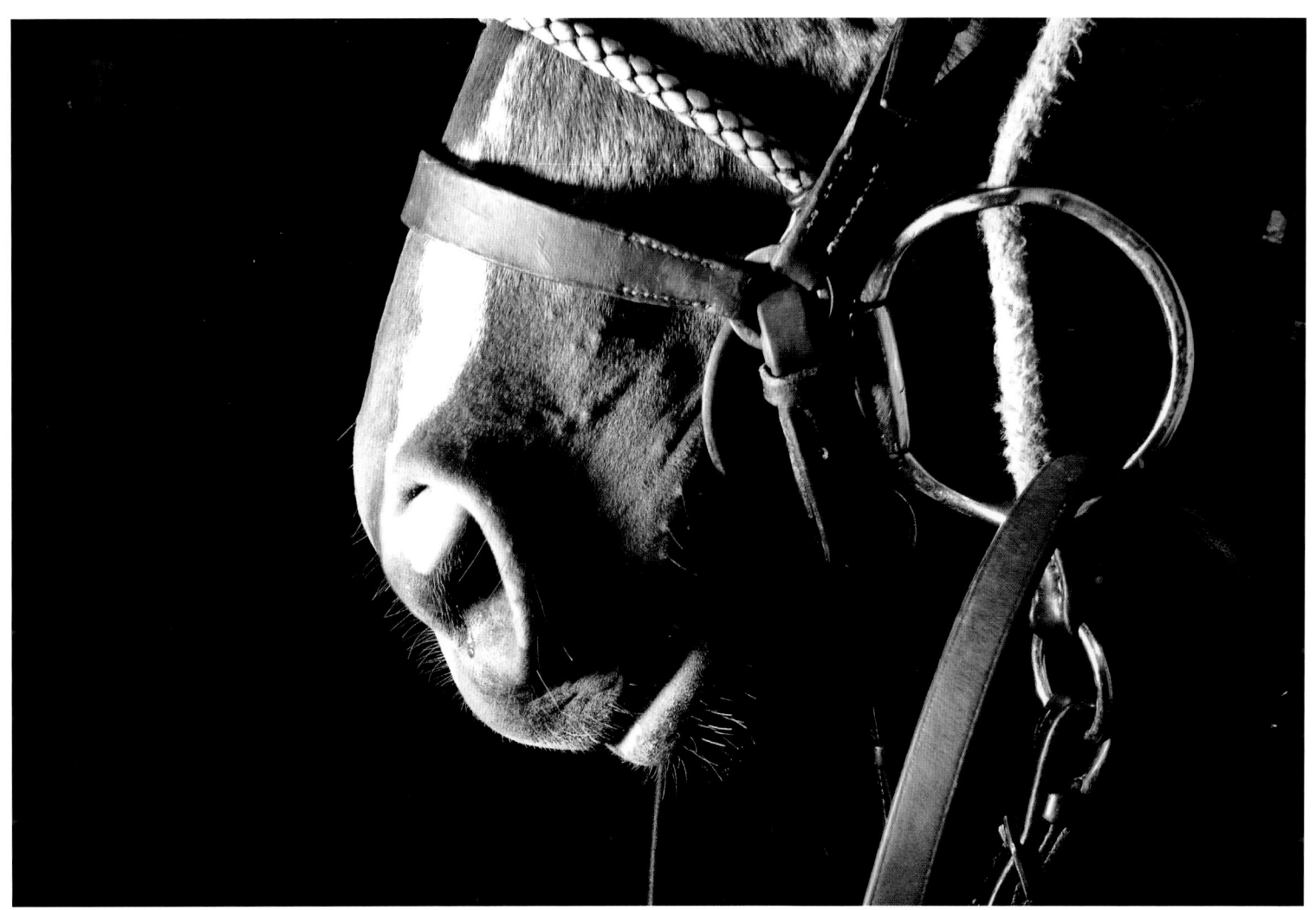

Incredibly fine detail reproduction

7.   On the Road
The High Art of Street Photography

Why did you buy a Leica M? And did you come across the images of Henri Cartier-Bresson and Alex Webb accidentally or deliberately?

You will have noticed by now that I often refer to photographers who are members of the Magnum agency. This is because there is no other agency in the world that concentrates so singe-mindedly on photos of real-world experiences, and not only in war zones and disaster areas. Photographers like Henri Cartier-Bresson and Alex Webb have photographed their fair share of wars and disasters while they and others, such as Thomas Hoepker, Constantine Manos, and René Burri, to name just a few, have been instrumental in putting the art of street photography on the map. Many Magnum photographers still shoot their street photos using cameras decorated with a red dot.

What is street photography? Although the term seems to infer an unsystematic approach to taking pictures, good street photography always has a strong underlying concept.

Here too, you need to work out in advance what you want to achieve. If, like Elliott Erwitt, you want to photograph dogs, you are better off at the beach or in a park than you are in a café where dogs aren't allowed. If you want to follow in Alex Webb's footsteps and create a book about Istanbul or some other city, you need to know as much background as possible about the culture and the lay of the land at your chosen location. You will also need to plan more than one trip.

Many of the photos in my German Angst series are typical street shots; so let's take a look at how I go about planning such a project.

In this case, I began by looking for subjects that fit in with the notions of German hesitancy and fastidiousness that are the heart of the project. I wanted to create images without inherent prejudice that allow viewers to form their own opinions. I researched upcoming events that I hoped would provide stimulating material, thus giving myself a timeline and a specific target. The events I selected included the Karneval (Mardi Gras) celebrations in Cologne, anti-nuclear demonstrations and the defusing of a wartime bomb. I shot on foot, from my car, and from the train, capturing portraits and images of landscapes and spaces, some with and some without people as their main subject. In all the towns I visited I shot from above and below, sometimes using deliberate blur or under- and overexposure. Some of the situations I planned simply didn't materialize, but I also captured many images that I hadn't reckoned on at all. My research and my targeted approach furnished me with the luck I needed. On some days, I captured 10 really good pictures; on others I ended up with none.

Keep in mind that street photography requires concentration. You won't usually be able to shoot meaningful images on a Sunday stroll, although you should always have your Leica with you.

How to Approach People

Planning a shoot also helps you to overcome the reluctance most people feel when asking strangers for permission to take photos. Have you ever missed a photo opportunity because you didn't dare ask? Don't worry; you aren't alone.

Whether you are working on your own a predetermined plan or on an assignment given to you by someone else, having a specific aim in mind will make it much easier to approach people and explain what you are doing and why.

It is also easier to photograph strangers if you spend time with them first and build a rapport. Imagine you are shooting at a fishing port. You could simply approach the first fisherman you see and ask if you can go ahead and take some pictures, or you could spend some time looking around with your camera on prominent display and wait to see if someone speaks to you or reacts to your presence. It doesn't really matter how you create a situation, the important thing is to take the plunge.

In street photography it is important to react quickly, so you need to have your camera ready at all times with aperture and shutter speed set and the lens focused to infinity. You can also use the depth-of-field scale on your lens to pre-focus. Use a moderate wide-angle lens, stop down to f/8 (or even smaller), and focus on your chosen area while making sure the distance setting you select lies between the two f/8 markings on the lens, and you can now shoot within your own predetermined range without having to refocus at all.

Photo Exercise #7

Take your camera and just one lens; a 28mm, 35mm, or 50mm. Using only this lens, look for a small, manageable location such as a farmer's market, a fishing harbor, or a popular plaza, and create a story in just five strong images.

The Hamburg Harley Days

The Hamburg Harley Days is a major event that divides opinion in the city like no other. For some it is simply too loud and brash, while others see it as a fun time that is good for local business. While I admit it does get really loud at times, I like the color and variety the bikers bring to town.

The main event takes place on an unattractive industrial plot where markets are held. The photo opportunities there are fairly limited. The real action happens on Hamburg's famous Reeperbahn red-light drag, an area that is full of bars, clubs, theaters, restaurants, and brothels. Reeperbahn is a four-lane street with a large square on the south side where the bikers gather to see and be seen, race their bikes, and indulge in the obligatory burnouts. This is the place to be if you want to document the true nature of the event. For this story, I used two main shooting techniques: the "flash with under-exposed background" technique I described in the previous chapter and a panning technique. For close-up shots, the first technique worked well, however, my flash wasn't powerful enough to illuminate long-distance scenes of the bikers riding by. For those shots, I wanted to convey the speed involved without generating too much blur and confusion. The best way to suppress busy backgrounds in situations like this is to pan the camera during the exposure. I pre-focused on a suitable point on the street, framed the bikes in the viewfinder, and shot using shutter speeds between 1/30 second and 1/60 second while following the movement with the camera. These two very different photographic styles complement each other perfectly.

All the photos reproduced here were captured using my M8 with 28mm and 35mm lenses.

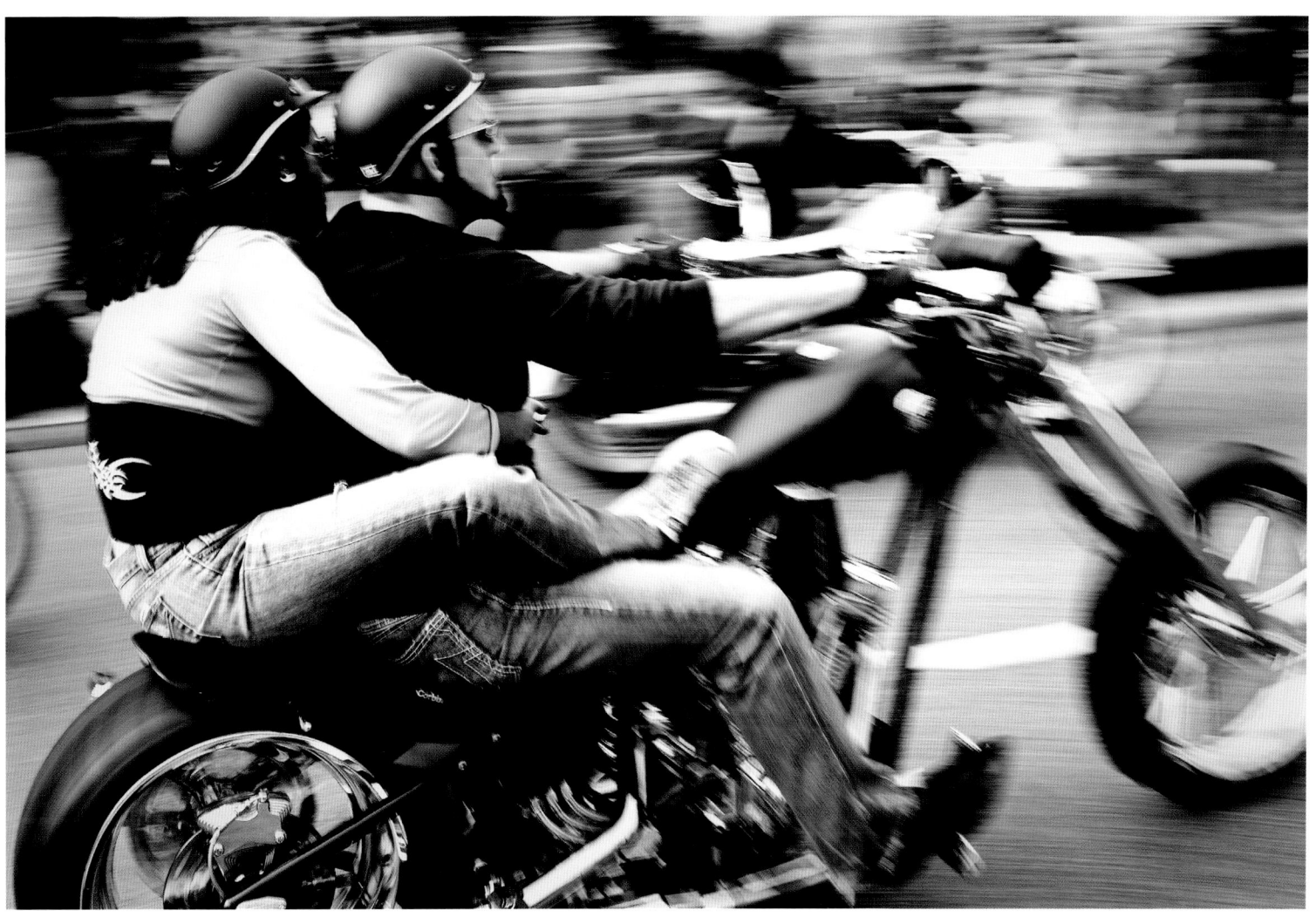

Check out the passenger's footrests

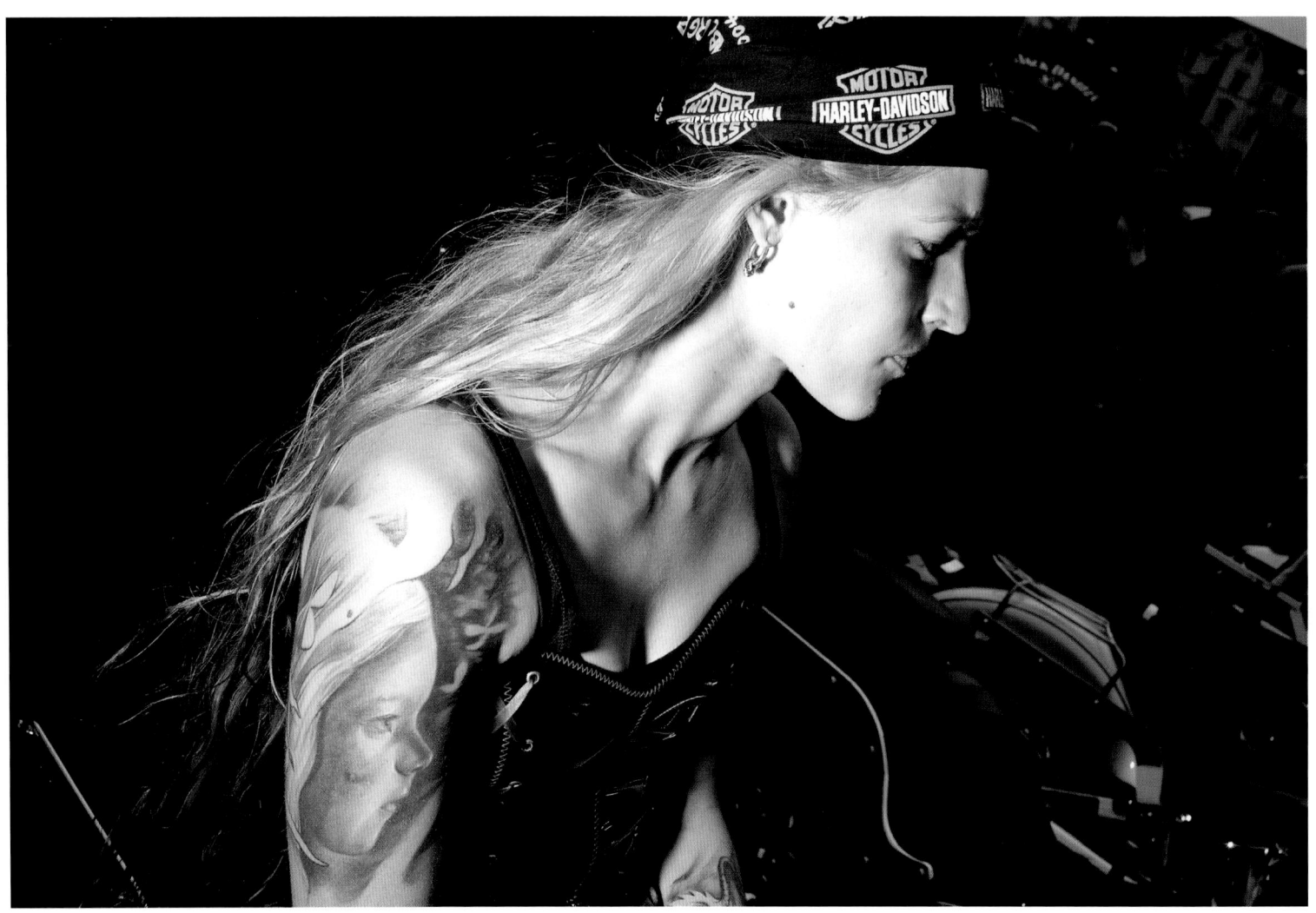

This woman's bandanna leaves no doubts about her allegiances

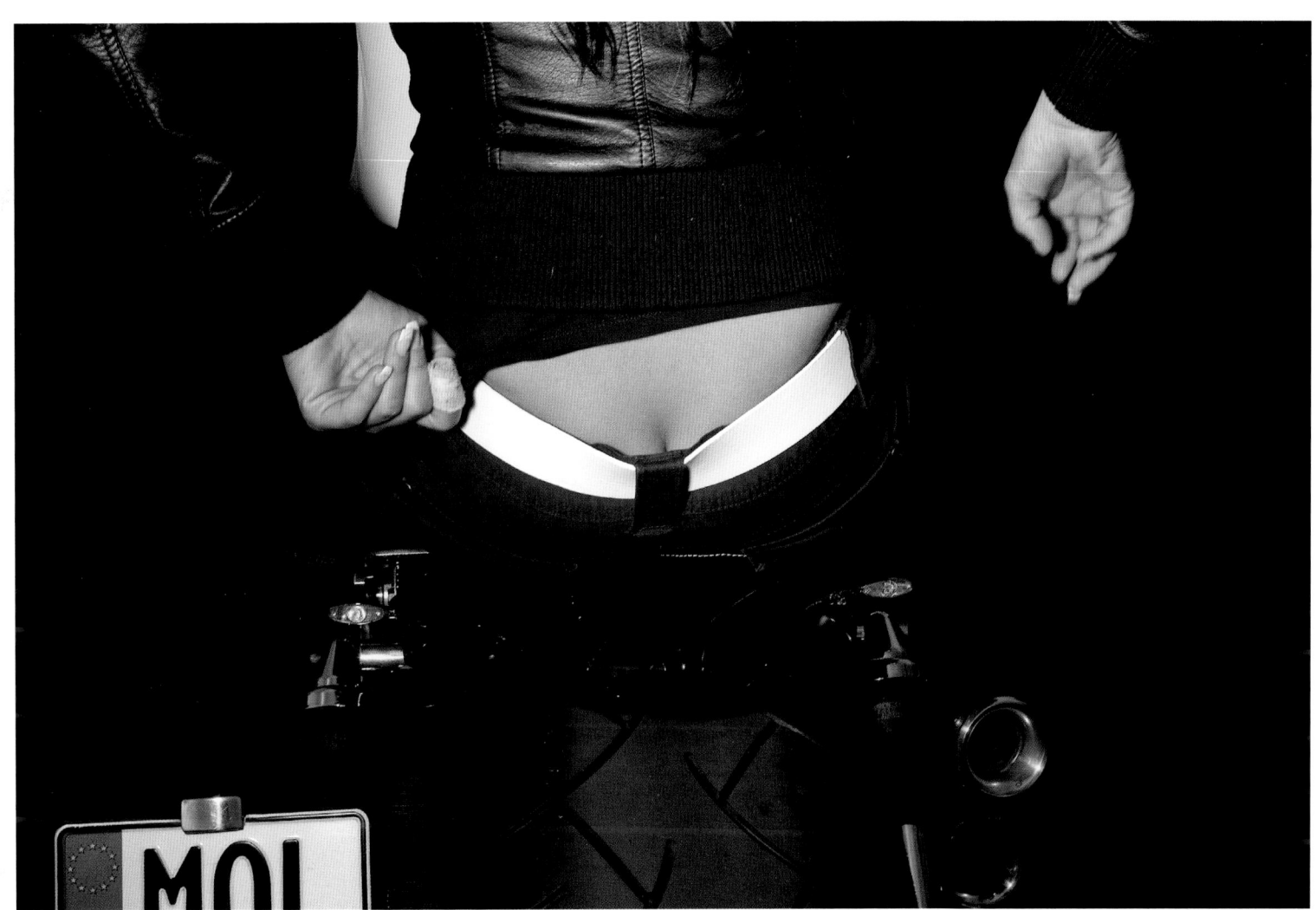

A rear view has a charm all its own

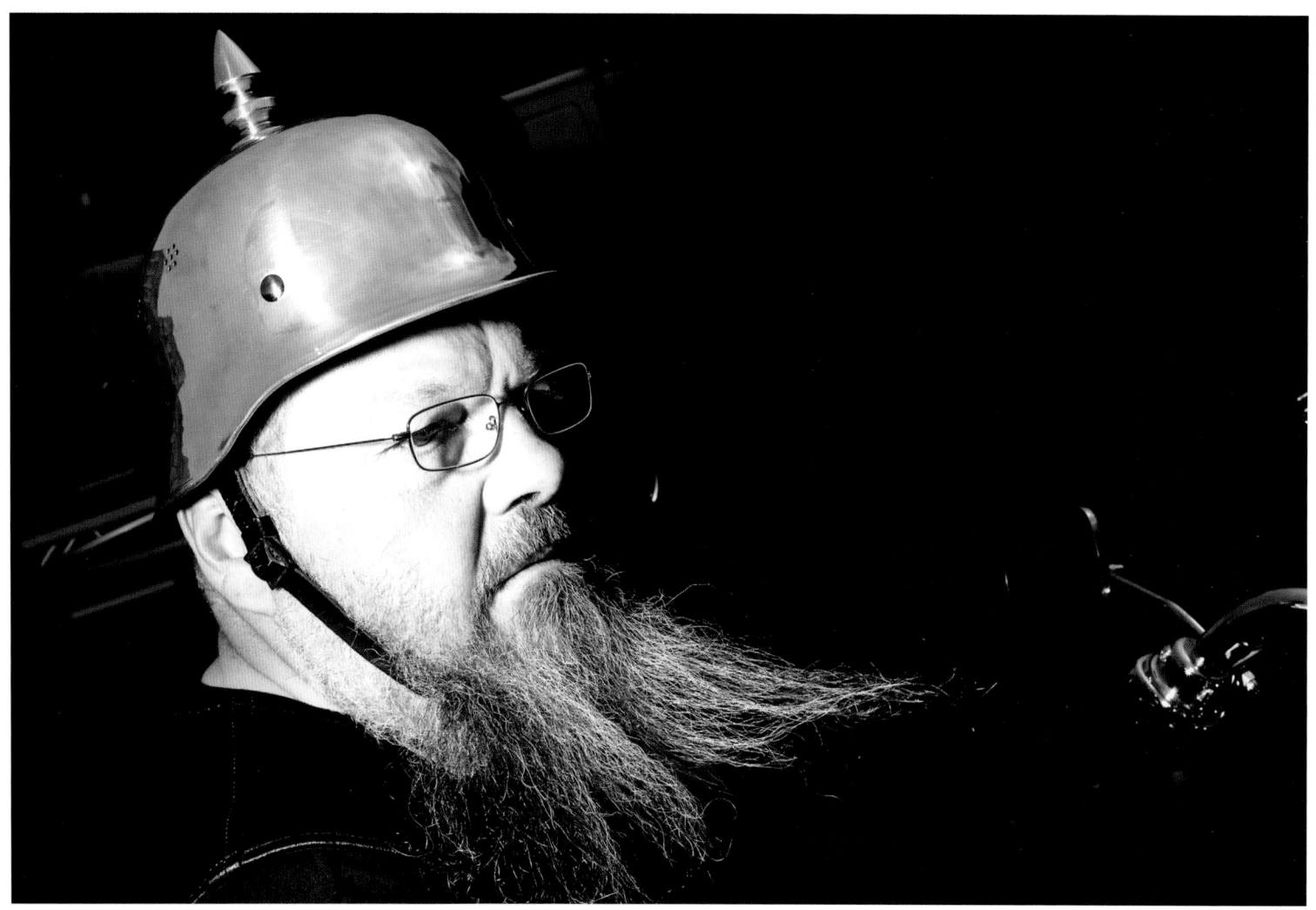

Head-to-toe styling

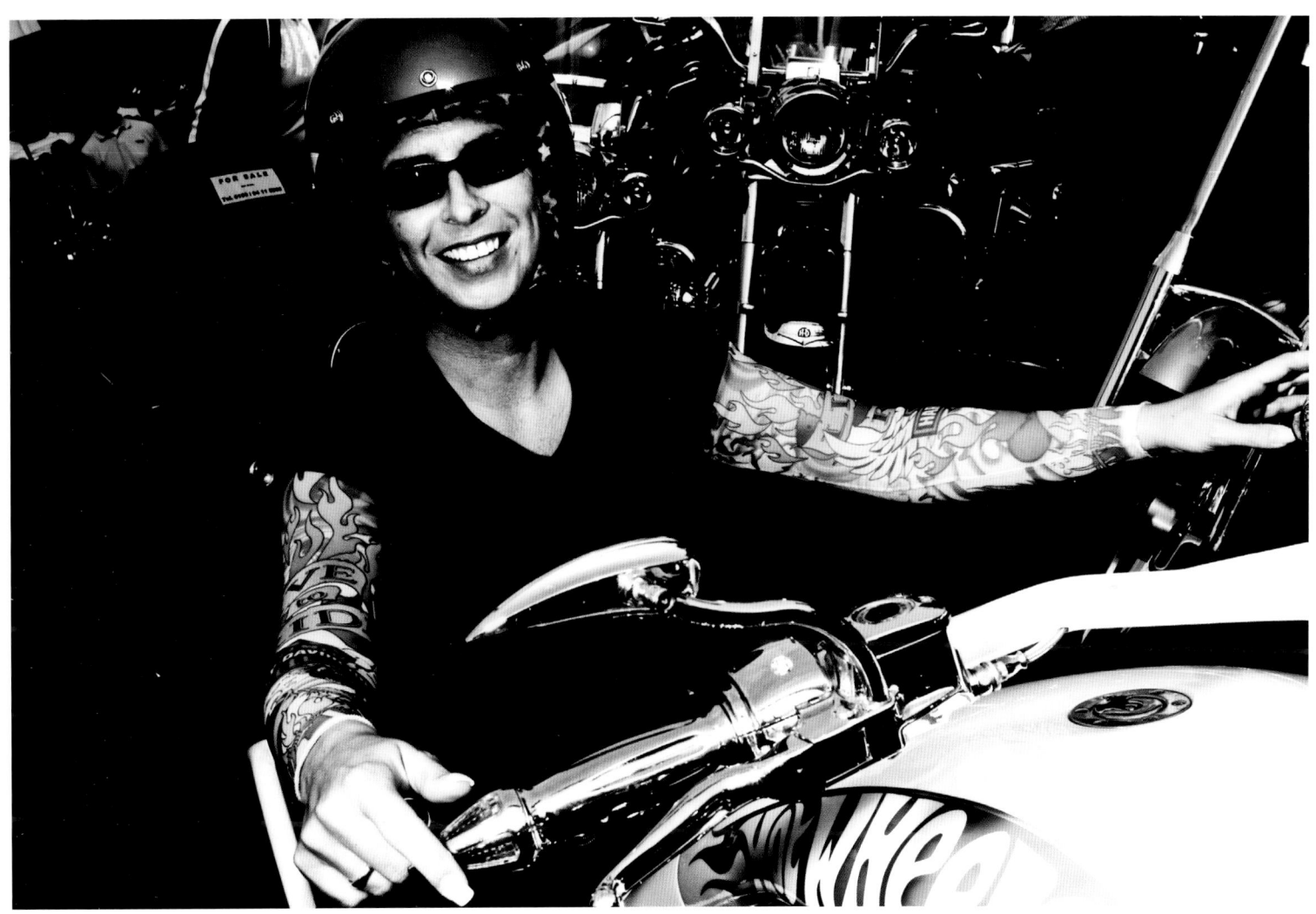

The shining chrome of the bikes in the background adds depth to this already appealing image

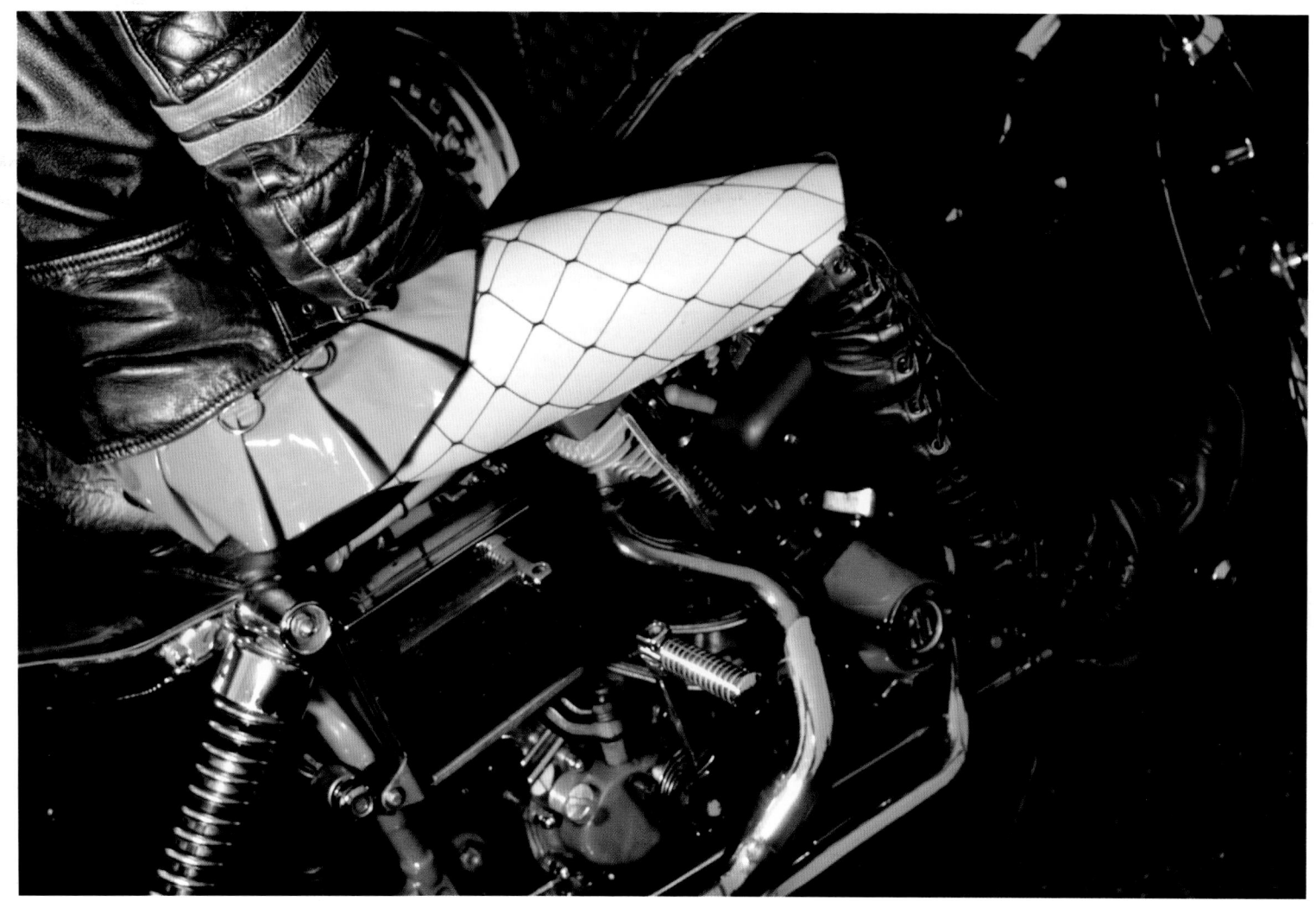

The bikes aren't the only things on display

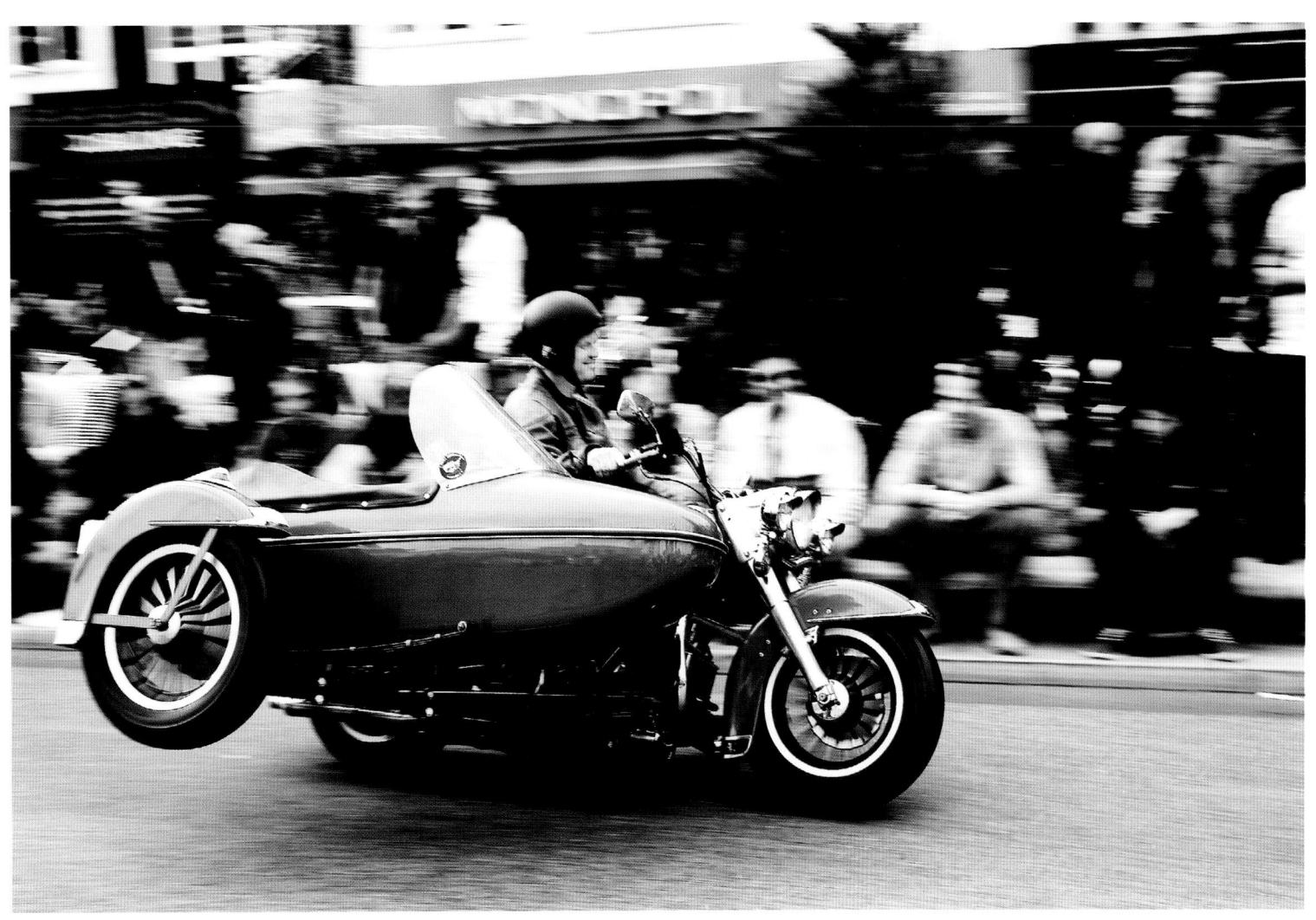

Acrobatics on wheels are part of the show

8. Trash

Selecting the Right Images

You just got home with a fine set of images and here I am talking about which ones to throw away. "Kill your darlings" is a phrase often heard among photographers, and perfectly describes the dilemma we face when selecting images. It goes without saying that you will discard obviously blurred and poorly exposed photos, or portraits in which the subject's eyes are half closed. Such images are not even second best and definitely belong in the trash.

How to Classify the Rest

When it comes to selecting images, all photographers have to overcome their own subjectivity. We tend to attribute a degree of quality to photos that is roughly commensurate with the effort put forth in capturing them. An insignificant snap can suddenly appear important if you walked a mile or climbed 400 steps to shoot it. Using complex gear, too, can make visual results seem weightier than they really are.

So, how can we work around our own preconceptions and avoid errors in judgment? If you are not working against a deadline, it's a great help to simply wait. I find that images I consider to be good (or even great) when I view them immediately after a shoot have often lost their appeal when I review them a couple of weeks later. By that time, the effect of the effort involved in capturing the images has lessened and photos that are nothing special reveal their true character.

Unfortunately, you won't always have the luxury of waiting a month before you make a selection, so experienced but impartial help is essential. My best judge is my wife. If I am undecided about whether to keep an image, I can be sure my wife will give me an honest opinion without the slightest consideration for my feelings! Luckily, she is also able to explain why she thinks a particular image isn't up to snuff.

You can ask other photographers to help you too, but don't be disappointed if their comments aren't always positive, especially if you are working hard to develop your own style. Photographers often find it difficult to acknowledge the value of other styles, so you need to find open-minded people who have a genuine interest in your work. Comments like "It's never been done that way before" or "I've never seen anything like that" don't rate as qualified feedback.

If you post your photos on a social network, the comments you receive will often be skewed. The fact is, if you don't dispense enough "likes" to others, you won't get "liked" back. People with extensive networks of "friends" collect plenty of "likes," regardless of the quality of the work they show. The other problem with social networks is that the people who post the most get more attention than others. Legitimate opinions tend to get drowned out in the noise.

Having said all that, online discussions about photographers and photography can be enlightening. Some images get slammed because the photographer has managed to produce something unusual;

also, legitimate compositions can quickly become objects of derision. Such discussions often have nothing to do with the content of the images or the stories they tell and instead concentrate almost entirely on superficial visual effects.

A good example of a discussion getting derailed was the one surrounding Jacob Aue Sobol's images of the Trans-Siberian Railway, shot for Leica using a pre-production M Monochrome. His gritty, high-contrast images gained him entry to the exclusive club of Magnum photographers but were the subject of heavy online criticism. As I followed the discussions, I had the distinct impression that as more critical comments were posted, more copycats joined the bandwagon. Challenges to these comments were simply brushed aside and the overriding tone of the discussion appeared to defend established values and to vilify an unfamiliar approach.

Professional photographers don't have it any easier. Many newspapers and magazines have strict guidelines concerning what they print and what they don't—a situation that often leads to dull publications without a hint of variety.

Despite the criticism your work might receive, I encourage you to break away from the norm and to experiment with new ideas.

Select 10 photos from a pool of at least 100 and get one or two friends to make their own selections.

Compare the images you each have chosen and discuss your reasons for making the choices you did.

Make 10 prints and show them to five people. Try to find out who likes or dislikes which images and why. The comments you receive are sure to be just as distinctively individual as the people making them.

The Karneval in Cologne

While selecting the images for this book, I discovered that I prefer to shoot my own private stories in black-and-white. I don't really know why this is, although it could be because 95 percent of my commissioned work is in color. Or do I simply prefer to avoid the challenges that shooting in color presents? The images shown here come from a side project that ensued from my *German Angst* work. I was traveling around the country around the time of Shrove Monday in 2012 putting some of my ideas into practice and, as always when I am on the road and working in "wide awake" mode, plenty of unplanned opportunities were presented to me on a platter.

The Karneval celebrations in Cologne were the final highlight of my tour. Hotel prices in Cologne shoot up around Karneval time, so I drove to Cologne on the morning of Shrove Monday and left my car in a parking lot were I knew I would be able to leave that evening without getting snarled up in traffic. I shot within a 500-yard radius of the famous Cologne cathedral and concentrated on capturing "darker" images for my *German Angst* series alongside the colorful antics of the partygoers. This wasn't an easy balancing act, but I think I managed to switch successfully between the two concepts. It was certainly easier than when I used to shoot with two analog cameras loaded with different types of film. On such occasions, I always seem to end up capturing my planned color images with my black-and-white camera and my monochrome ideas in color.

The images reproduced here were all captured using my M9 with 35mm and 50mm lenses.

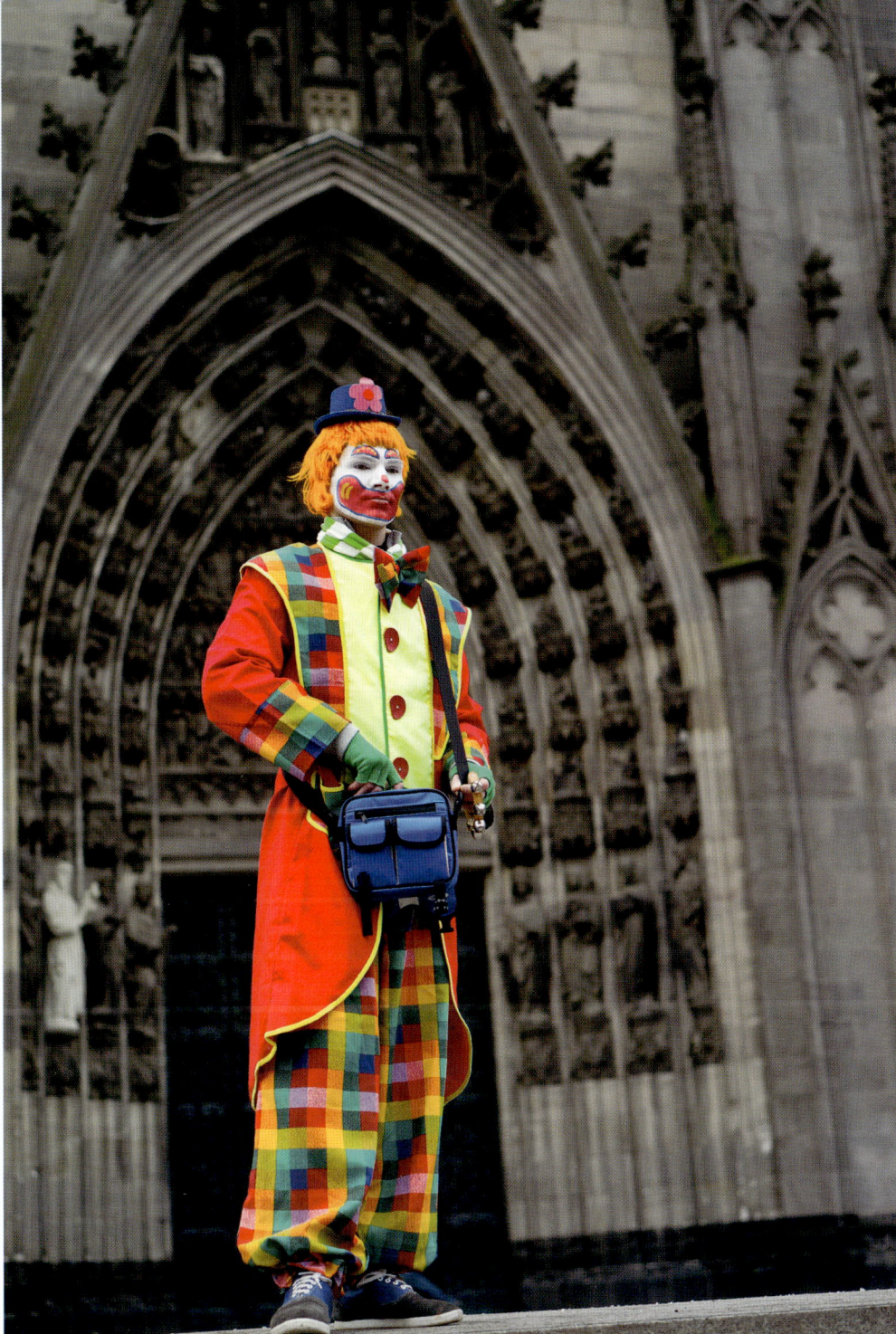

The colorful nature of the clown's costume is underscored by the monochrome background, and the cathedral door frames the subject perfectly

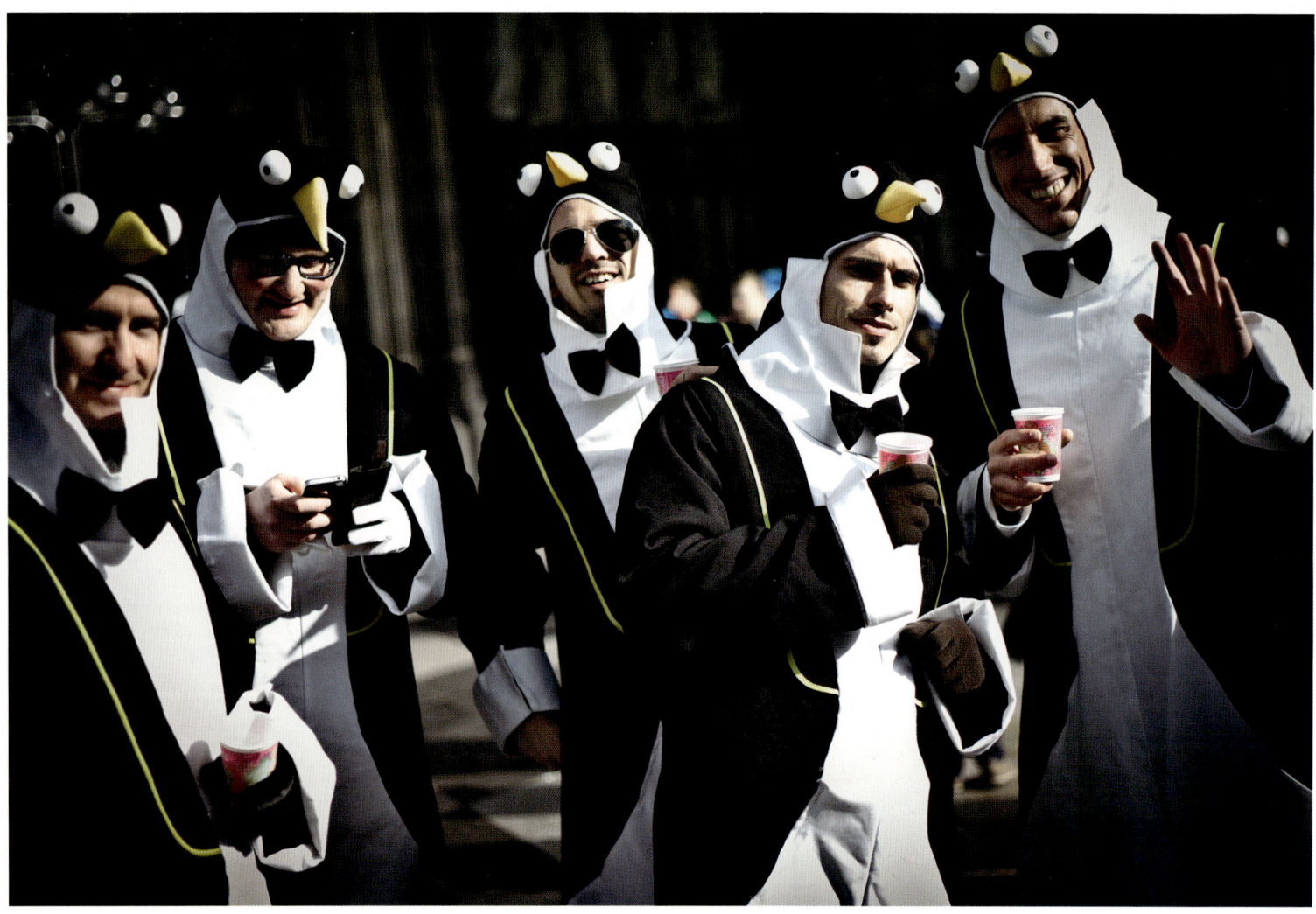

The effectiveness of this image revolves around the limited number of colors it contains

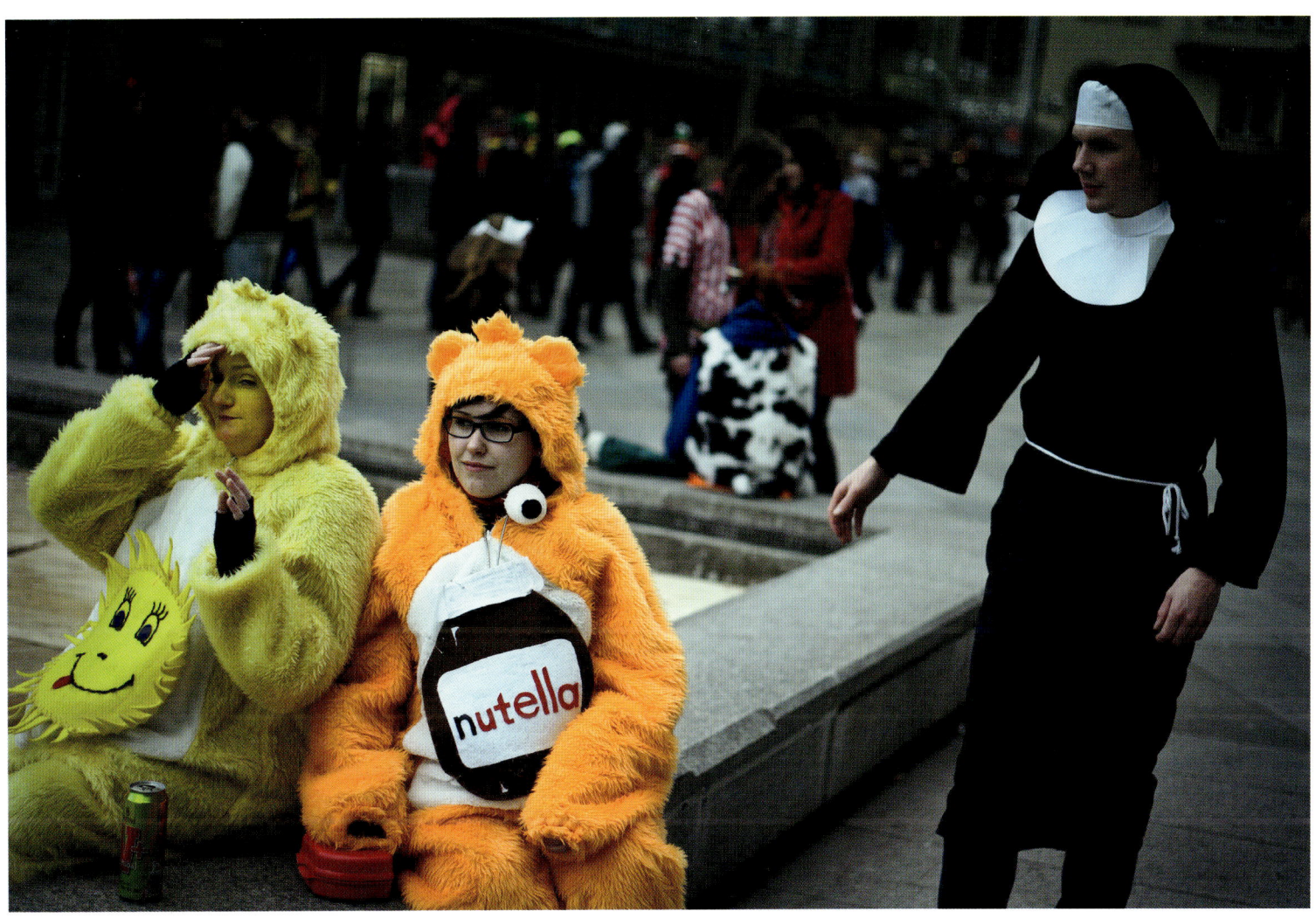

This is simply funny

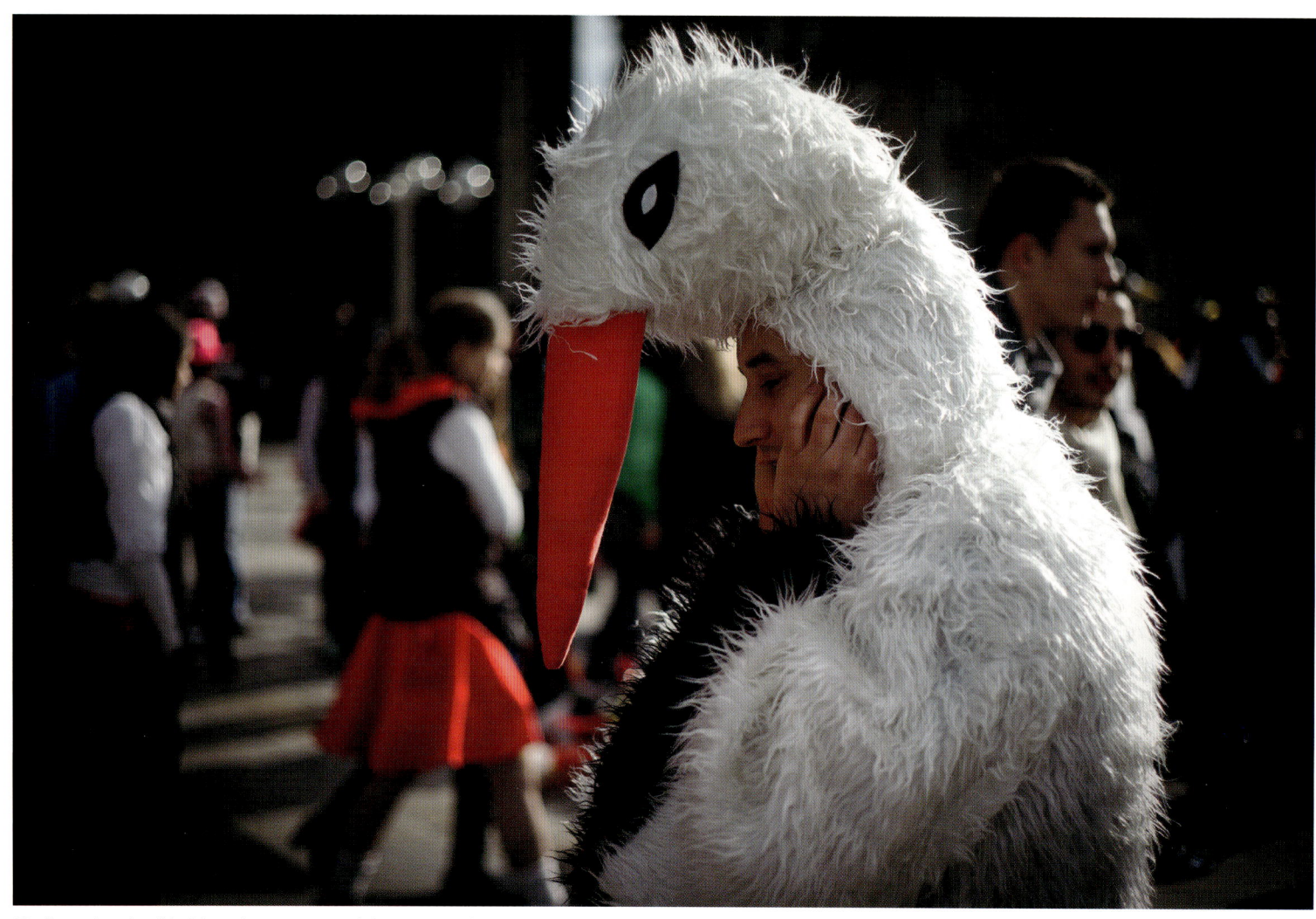

Shallow depth of field and repetition of the main colors in the background draw the viewer in

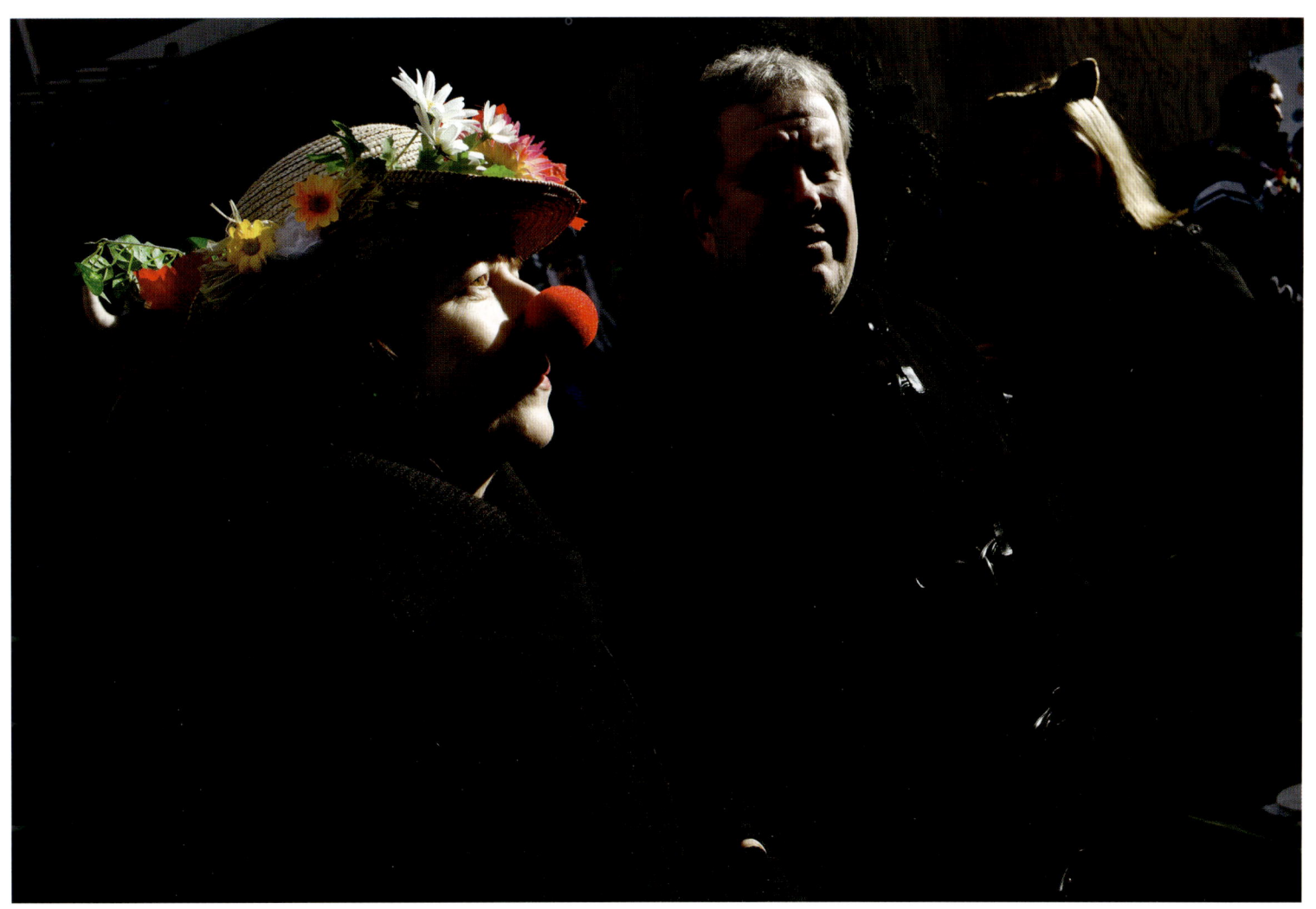

Deliberate use of the low late-afternoon sun and suppression of shadow detail give this image the necessary punch

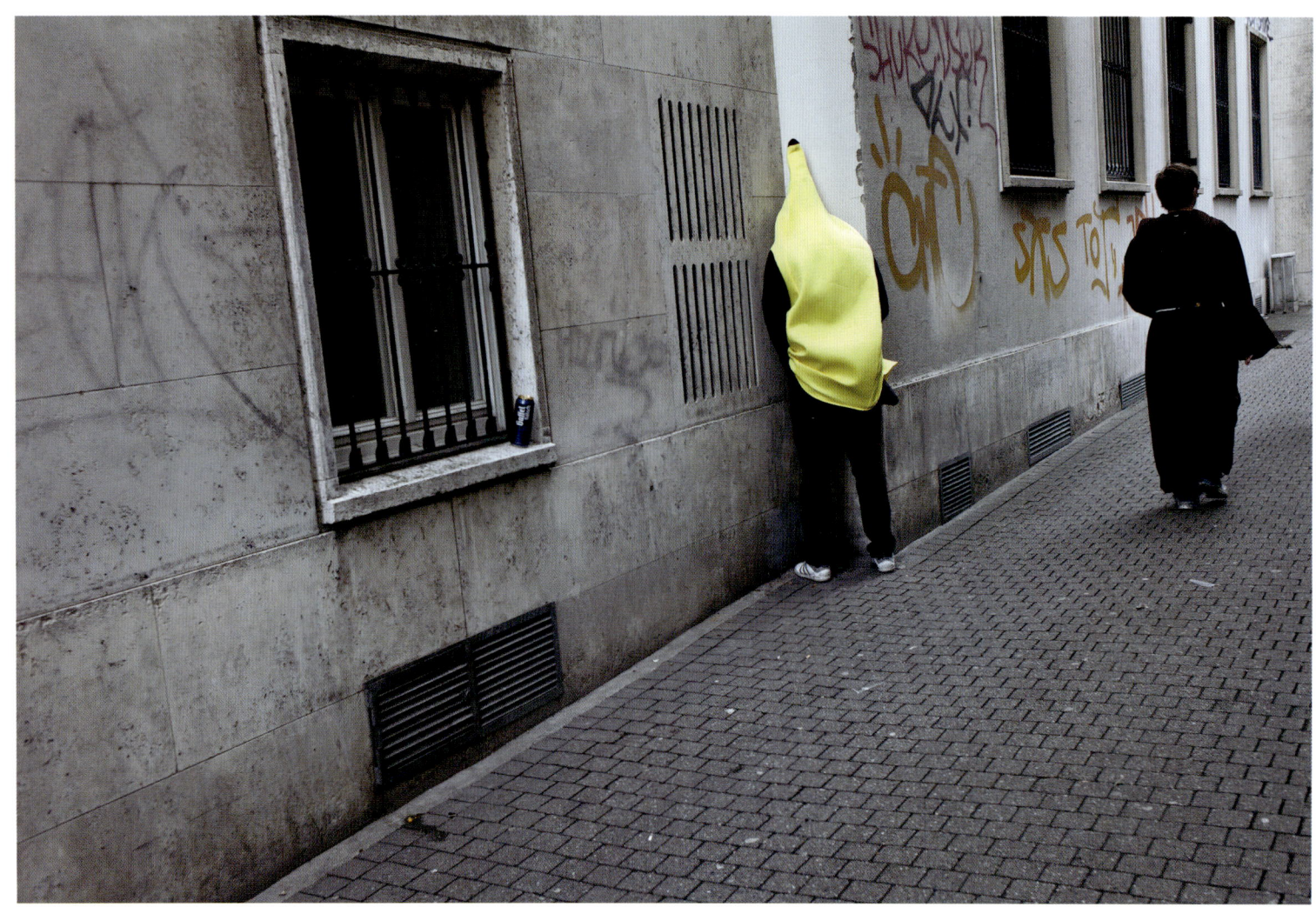

A monochromatic color image in which a banana relieving himself is the most conspicuous detail!
The less prominent "monk" underscores the humor of the situation.

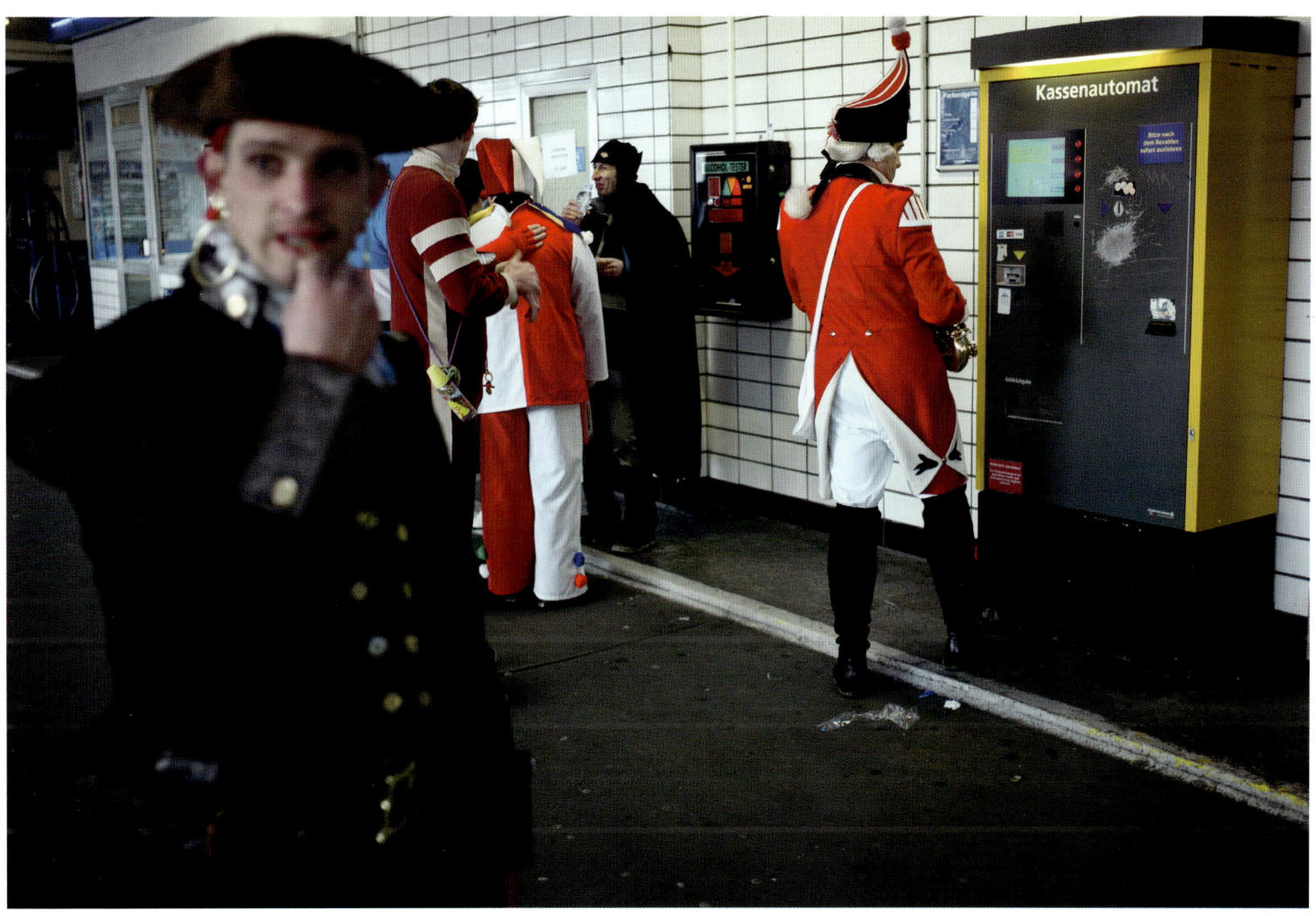

Back to reality at the car park. The success of this image relies on the presence of the gentleman in the foreground.

9. In the Darkroom
The Pros and Cons of Image Processing

Do we really need to process our digital images? To shoot with an analog camera, you have to select a film that suits the project at hand: either black-and-white or color (negative or slide). You can also choose between various brands and different film sensitivities. At the development stage, you can influence the look of black-and-white negatives by altering the strength and temperature of the developer fluid or the duration of the process. Slide film can also be developed with negative developer using a technique called cross-processing. And after you have developed your film, the enlargement and printing process offers you choices of hard or soft paper with a plastic or Baryta substrate.

Even in these digital times, analog techniques are still held by many to be the benchmark for authentic photography, although alongside the processing possibilities listed above, blatant forgeries, too, have always been a regular feature of the everyday photo workflow. In analog times, people and places were grafted into and sliced out of images, and details that existed in negatives were often simply dodged to the point of invisibility or burned until they were unrecognizable.

I know plenty of sports photographers who inserted "missing" footballs into their prints and many were never found out. Limiting yourself to making digital manipulations of the kinds that were possible in the analog darkroom doesn't guarantee authentic results. Of course, it is a lot easier to manipulate images digitally, but photographic fabrications have been around as long as photography itself.

The digital equivalent of an analog negative is a RAW image file

The Digital Darkroom

I have to break my promise about treating analog and digital Leica photographers equally. Most analog photographers choose whether to shoot in color or black-and-white by selecting an appropriate film before the shoot even begins, whereas (with the exception of the Leica M Monochrome) digital photographers can leave this decision until later. I say "can" because I prefer that you think in advance how you want your results to look. Black-and-white photography isn't just color photography with the color taken out; and although an average-quality color image can sometimes gain impact if you convert it to monochrome, it will rarely become really good regardless of how you process it.

In a color photo, the composition and the colors have to form a harmonious whole, and it is rare that images benefit from kitschy colors. Gaudy colors can be fun but usually make an image look overblown. Successful color images usually contain either repeated tones, subtle tones, or carefully positioned signal colors.

The most important elements of a black-and-white image are the nuances that exist between the various grayscale shades it contains and its contrast.

In the digital darkroom, you can develop your images according to the look you have planned for them. Many news agencies have a written code of ethics regarding the processing steps their photographers are allowed to apply. If you take a look at the standards recommended by The Associated Press, you will find that the organization even frowns upon use of the anti-red-eye effects. Generally speaking, processing tools should only be used to subtly enhance attributes that are already present in an image, especially in documentary photography.

Even if you are not shooting for photojournalistic purposes, excessive post-production is usually counterproductive. High dynamic range (HDR) images created by merging a sequence of underexposed, correctly exposed, and overexposed images have become extremely popular in recent years and are, in my opinion, a great example of an impressive technique that quickly loses its appeal when overdone.

Your Leica is a fantastic tool that I hope will encourage you to shoot great images from the get-go, rather than average images that you can pep up later. Of course, all RAW images require a little processing, and the best option here is a powerful but intuitive all-in-one program like Adobe Lightroom, which is supplied with every new Leica. A well-thought-out photo will only require subtle post-processing to help it reveal its best qualities.

Photo Exercise #9

Select a scan or a photo file and try out as many different processing options as you can. Don't hold back; adjust the sliders as much as you like. Save each version and compare the results. The most highly processed image is not always the best, and you are sure to find that some combinations of processing steps produce more authentic-looking results than others.

Using Third-Party Lenses

Your choice of lens is another way to influence the look of an image. Although the current crop of Leica lenses offers high-quality reproduction characteristics, some legacy models produce results with a more distinctive look. Some lenses produce obvious vignetting effects, while others produce soft-looking images when used wide open or at short distances. Optically speaking, such lenses aren't of the highest quality but are still capable of producing visually exquisite images if used correctly. There are plenty of highly respected images that were captured using crude pinhole cameras, providing further proof that the concept and the quality of execution are just as important as technical perfection when it comes to creating great photographs.

I love to test the technical limits of my gear. As you can see from the photos in this book, I like to shoot at wide apertures, and the brighter the lens the more fun this is.

Voigtländer and Zeiss are the best-known manufacturers of third-party lenses equipped with the Leica M bayonet. While researching this book, I came across a number of photographers who use third-party lenses to achieve specific effects

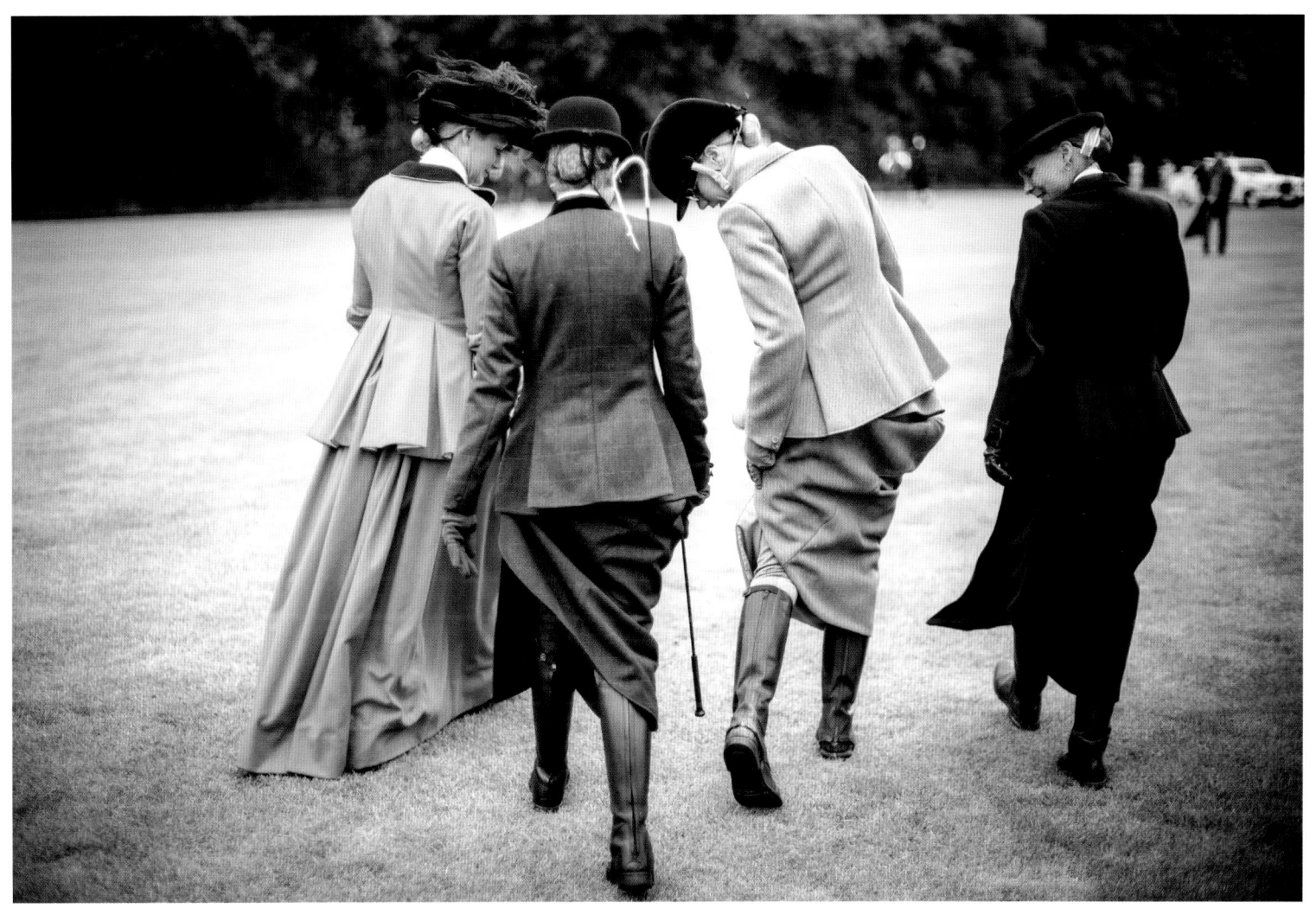

The ladies leaving the field of play

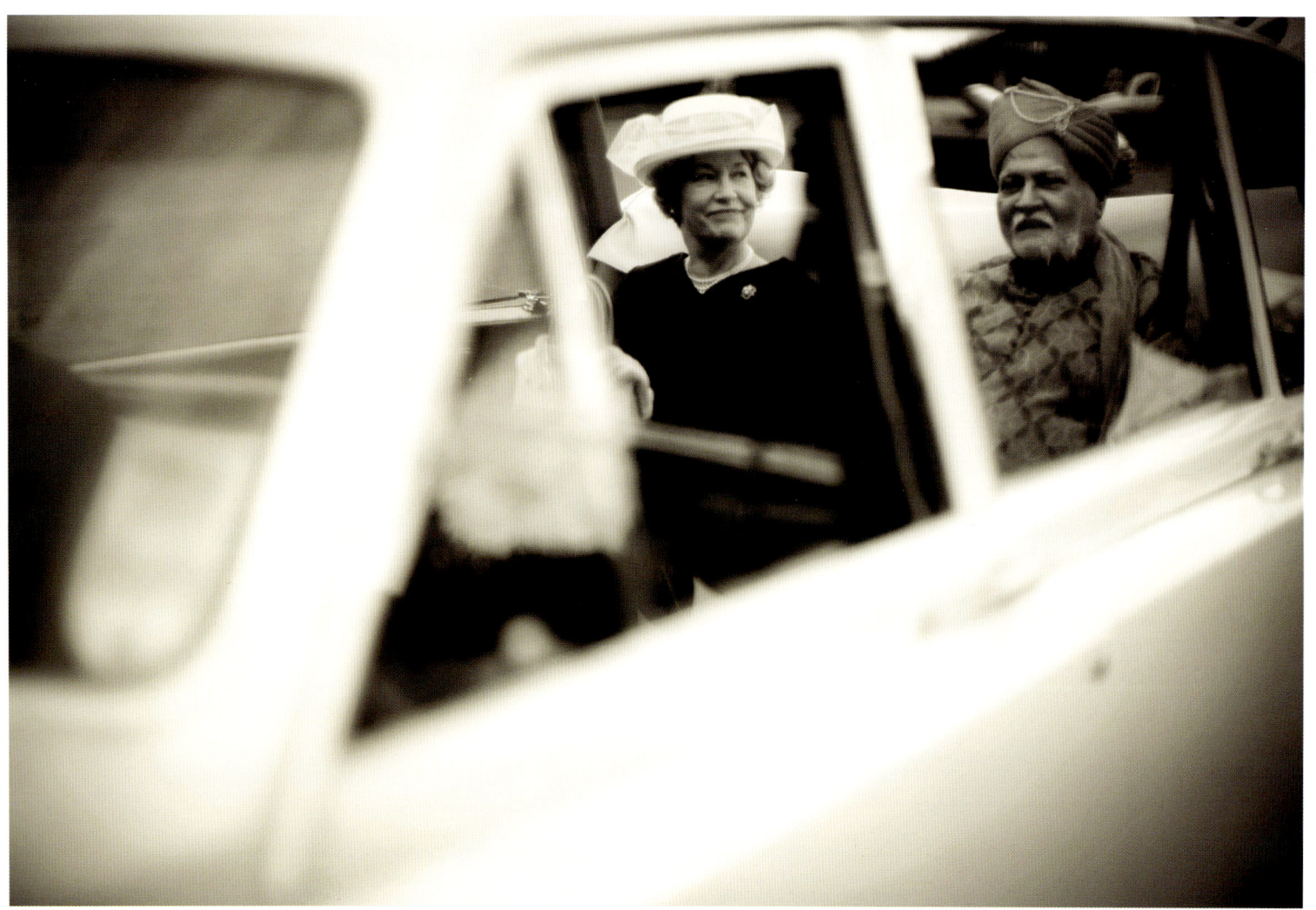

The "Queen" and her escort in a Daimler landaulet

with their Leicas. Jan Garup is a lovable and talented Danish photojournalist whose main lenses are highly specialized 35mm f/1.2 and 50mm f/1.1 Viogtlander Noktons, which he uses for his warzone photography.

His technique made me curious, so I approached Voigtländer with a tentative request for the loan of a lens or two. A couple of days later, four lenses landed on my desk. I don't need to explain how shallow the depth of focus is in an f/1.1 lens, but these lenses are still a dream to work with, even if I did end up producing more reject portraits and close-ups than usual.

This chapter's assignment took place at the annual British Days festival in Hamburg, which is visited mostly by Brits and Anglophiles. I used just the 35mm and 50mm Voigtländer lenses and shot exclusively at maximum aperture. I really love these lenses, even if they aren't appropriate for every scenario. I certainly have a few more ideas to test before I give them back!

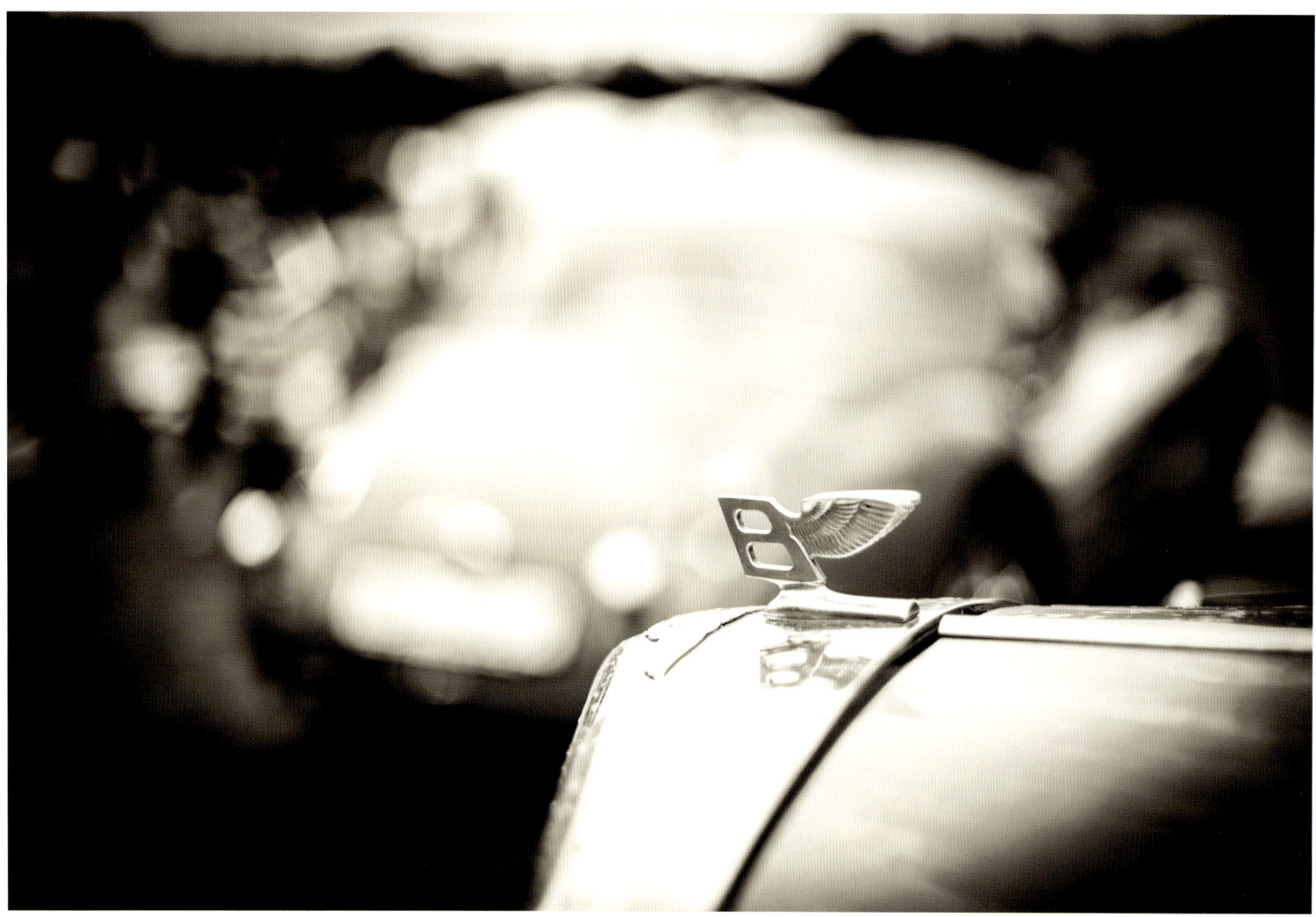

The Bentley wing with a convertible in the background

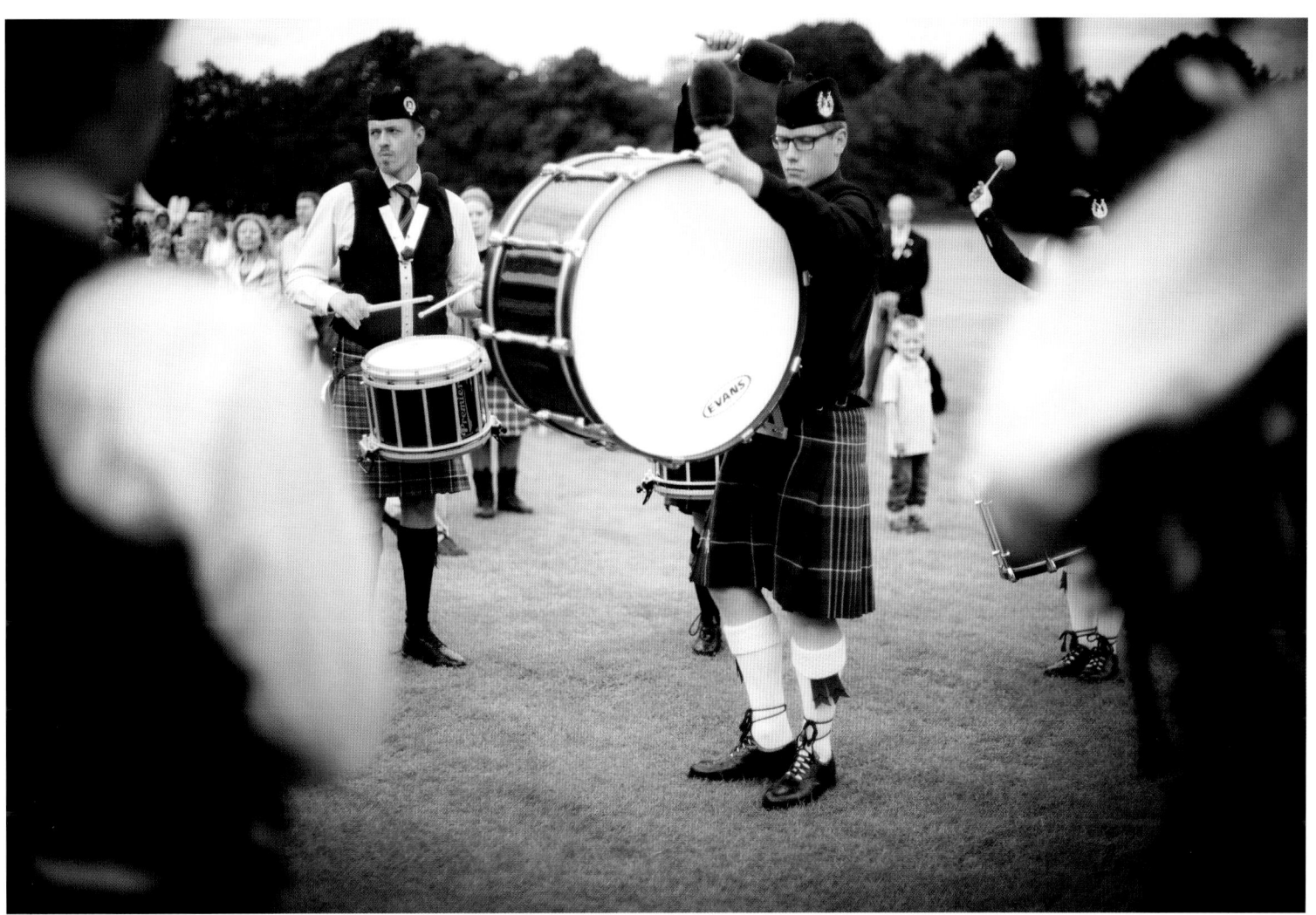

Pipe and drums enhance the mood of the day

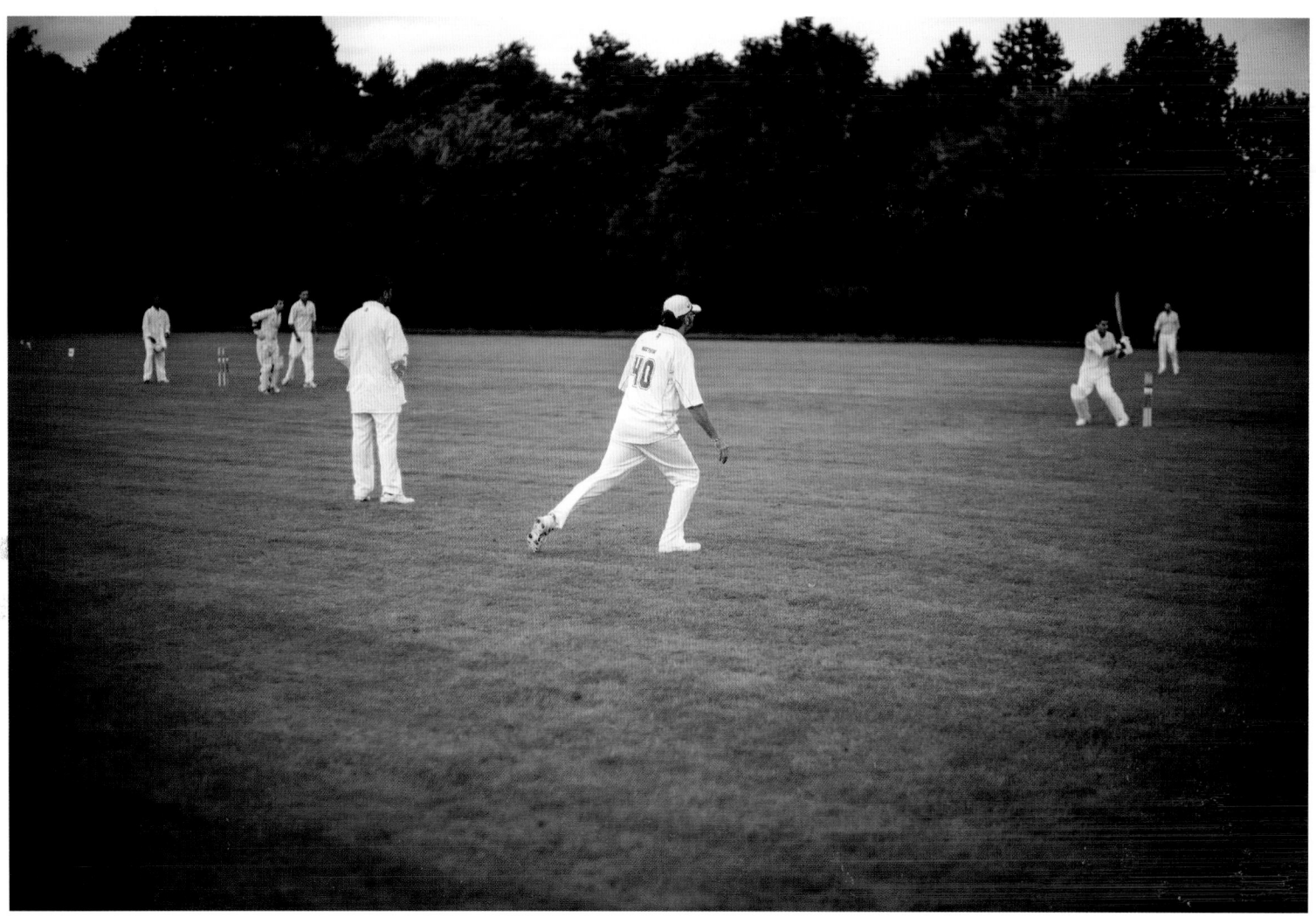

A game of cricket, shot from a distance to produce a pleasing graphic effect

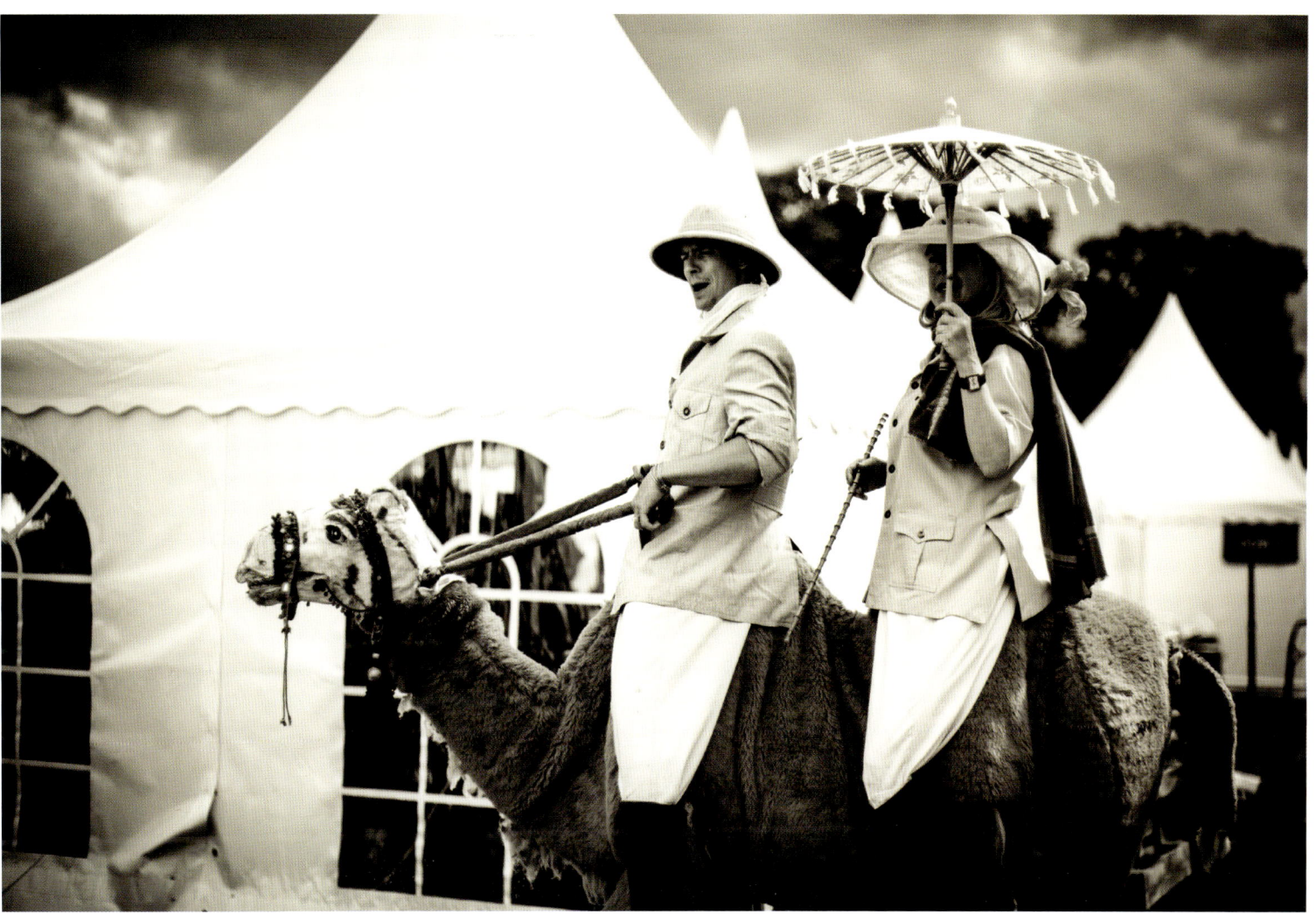

People being silly in front of silly-looking tents

10. Clothes Make the Person
How to Present Your Work

You have shot a sequence of images, made a selection from the results, and now you want to present your work to an eager public.

The reason Leica packs its new cameras in high-end wooden boxes is to increase the perceived value of the device contained within. You should do the same with your precious images: the more sumptuous the "packaging" the better they are likely to be received.

I am frequently asked to review other photographer's portfolios and to offer comments on the appearance of the individual images as well as on the method of the presentation. I am often astonished by how photographers approach the task of presenting their work. Some start apologizing before I have seen a single image, thus making it clear from the start that they haven't achieved what they set out to do. This kind of attitude produces a negative vibe that definitely doesn't improve the situation.

Others carry their photos or portfolios in a plastic bag from a discount supermarket, which immediately infers that the work itself is junk, even when this is not actually the case.

Another way to get your viewer to lose interest is to use a notebook computer and click your way through to the "Portfolio" folder stored in the "Stories" folder stored in the "This Year's Photos" folder, only to find that the viewing software you installed doesn't work. The final straw is asking the person you are trying to impress if they know how to get your computer to work.

These are all real-world scenarios that I have experienced, and they prove beyond all doubt that even world-class images don't stand a chance if you don't present them appropriately. But that's enough negative press. How should you go about doing things right?

There is, of course, no single "right" solution and the first thing you need to do is identify whom you are targeting. Do you just want to show your images to someone who will give you advice, or are you on the lookout for a potential buyer or client? If the person you are talking to is an imaging professional, you must prepare for the meeting differently than if you are showing your images to a friend or neighbor.

Let's Look at Some Options

If you are showing prints, make sure none are smaller than 5" x 7". Unless you are advanced at printing images, always get your prints made at a professional lab, not at the drugstore. The only time you can use low-grade prints is if you are planning a book or an exhibition, but I will go into more detail on that scenario later on.

Once you have selected a lab, test different paper types as well as sizes. Baryta papers often give black-and-white images extra punch, while glossy paper can add vibrancy to color images. If you present your images in individual sleeves in a portfolio, you don't have to worry about fingerprints. If, however, you prefer to present your images loose in a presentation box, you should provide cotton gloves for your viewers or have your prints made on non-glossy paper. Remember, too, that different paper qualities have varying effects on the people handling them.

You can buy ready-made portfolio cases and boxes from most well-stocked photo dealers or you can have a custom case made by a bookbinder.

A computer is an obvious choice when it comes to presenting photos. You can use a notebook, a tablet, or a smartphone, depending on whom you are presenting to. Even if a smartphone isn't the ideal format for showing a story to an editorial team, it is always better to be able to show your photos in some form should the opportunity arise unexpectedly.

A notebook computer is a good choice as long as you know how to start a slideshow presentation using just a few clicks. If you have to fumble around with folders and operating systems, you will quickly lose your viewer's interest.

Tablet computers still exert a strong fascination for many people. If you have a high-end tablet, letting people swipe and pinch their way through your images is a fun way to get them involved in your work. Here too, you need top-notch software for this approach to be effective. And by the way, the Lightroom Printer menu includes options for adding borders, which can give portfolio images extra presence. Try to be as creative as possible in your presentations as well as in your everyday work.

Photo books are a surprisingly cheap and increasingly popular way to present photos. Most photo book services have their own user-friendly software that allows you to put together a book for individual or serial printing. You can build a book using your own graphics software as long as the service you use supports the format you produce.

Have you ever thought about putting on an exhibition but you didn't know whom to approach? It doesn't have to be a museum, since many cafés, bars, and doctor's offices put up temporary exhibitions and are happy to show work produced by locals. If I am planning an exhibition, I often make cheap drugstore prints of the images I have selected to check the effect they have when presented together. Shuffling a set of prints around on a tabletop is much easier than trying to judge their effect on a computer screen. I always carry a selection of postcards with my information on the front and at least five of my current images printed on the backs. I let the person I am talking to choose their favorite, thus giving them the opportunity to see some of my pictures and take away a small, high-quality gift. The person sees all five choices and then selects their favorite, thus I am provided with direct feedback on my work. An obvious bonus is that my card serves as a reminder of who I am and what I do.

A web presence is essential for anyone who wants to earn money from taking photographs—if you cannot be found on the Internet, you simply don't exist as a photographer. Unfortunately, many pros have not yet adapted to this aspect of modern marketing.

I update my website regularly and link the latest version to my Facebook and XING (a European social network for professionals similar to LinkedIn in the U.S.) profiles. I also upload small, low-res copies of my images to Facebook as a kind of running diary of my work.

I no longer use a physical portfolio because it simply involves too much effort. Nowadays, I use photo books to present my work to editorial teams and potential clients. This is a quick and relatively cheap way to produce a custom portfolio that you can give away at the end of the meeting. Many people are reluctant to throw away a book, so this approach often creates a lasting impression.

Remember: Creativity is key to every aspect of your work and should be part of your thought process from the initial concept up to the moment you present your images.

Thanks

This book only exists because of the support of the following people and the faith they showed in the project.

First and foremost I would like to thank my publisher, Gerhard Rossbach, for his boundless enthusiasm, without which the original concept would never have gotten off the ground.

Thanks too, to my editor [of the original German edition] Rudolf Krahm for motivating me and keeping me going when things got tough.

Special thanks go to Stefan Daniel, Andreas Dippel, Roland Ibrom and Jesko von Oeynhausen at Leica, who answered endless questions of varying intelligence and provided me with cameras and lenses that were, for all intents and purposes, not actually available. Gerd-Rainer Frost at Voigtländer gave me the opportunity to try out three ultra-bright lenses just before we finished work on the text.

Many thanks go to my countless "models." I hope you are not disappointed! Jan Kopp, owner of my favorite photo lab in Hamburg, produced many excellent exhibition-grade prints and even more small prints for me to send to the people in the photos.

And to you, dear Lutz Fischmann, Malte Gumpricht, Margot and Claus Harder, Lutz Rathenow, Carsten Rehder, Christiane Solcher, and Katja Solcher! It is thanks to your support and our innumerable discussions that I had the courage to start work on this book at all.

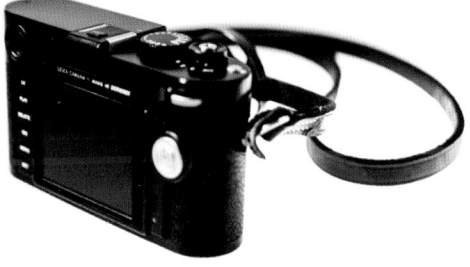